1978

WORDS
COME IN FAMILIES

EDWARD HOROWITZ, PH.D.

Illustrated by Harold Montiel

HART PUBLISHING COMPANY, INC. • NEW YORK CITY

DEDICATION

There are eleven of them—they are all bright and beautiful and have rare charm. They are the children of our children, and they fill these, the days of our later years, with sunshine and laughter.

They come in three groups:

Adina, Akiva, Ilana, and Aryeh Shalom are the children of Tamar and Victor Kagan.

Orli, Atara, and Chananel are the children of Sara and Carmi Horowitz.

Avigail, Elchanan, Michal, and Gilad Yosef are the children of Hadasa and Laurence Lewis.

This book is for them.

And, of course, for Jonathan, our youngest son.

CONTENTS

A FEW WORDS OF THANKS

All my life I have enjoyed playing with words. I would like to record these few words of grateful thanks to some books and some men who have contributed to my joy in word play and to the production of this book.

First of all, there is the Oxford English dictionary. If its thirteen large volumes are too much, consider the excellent one volume *The Oxford Dictionary of English Etymology* by C.T. Onions. Eric Partridge's *Origins* is a brilliant and exciting book. The two volumes of Ernest Klein's *A Comprehensive Etymological Dictionary of the English Language* published by Elsevier, constitute one of the most important contributions to English etymology in our generation.

My interested family all contributed generously of their talents. My daughter Tamar Kagan typed the entire manuscript. Her husband Victor Kagan, who teaches English at the Hebrew University, wrote many of the illustrative sentences, and gave me the benefit of his experience in teaching English as a foreign language. My wife Silvia, with her sure feel for words and keen editorial sense, always responded to my incessant questions. She really had very little choice.

The editorial department of the Hart Publishing Company, Beatrice Hart in particular, is responsible for the charming format of the book and for many felicitous and original suggestions. The artist Harold Montiel really made the words that he illustrated come alive.

I am very grateful to all these, and to my family and good friends.

EDWARD HOROWITZ

INTRODUCTION

A few words to the gentle reader
and to those who gladly teach:

English words come in families, great big beautiful and usually interesting families. As you turn these pages, we hope that you will see how beautiful and interesting English words can be.

You should look almost any English word squarely in the eye and ask this interesting question: *Why do you mean what you mean?*

Take the word EXTRACTION. We know that "ex" means *out;* "tract," *to draw;* and "tion," *the act of;* so that the whole word very simply means *the act of drawing out.*

Or take the word REPORTER. You know that "re" means *back;* "port," *to carry;* and "er" is *one who;* so that the whole word means *one who carries something* (in this case, news) *back.*

Now you might go on and ask—Yes, but why does "port" mean *to carry?* Why does "tract" mean *to draw, to pull?*

There is no answer to this question. "Port," and "tract" are among the root words of the English language. What does it mean to say that a word is a root? It means we do not know *why* it means what it means.

Please look at these root words with a very healthy respect. They stand in solitary splendor. They are the great building blocks of the English language. Regard them lovingly; each root can be the parent of a very large number of words—words that help you express the important thoughts that course through your brain.

The Origin of Language

You might wonder—how did language originate? It is very important that you know. There happens to be a very simple answer. WE DO NOT KNOW. It all happened so long ago that it is virtually impossible for men ever to wrest this secret from the shadowy past. Primitive men needed desperately to communicate with each other, to warn each other of danger, to express their common wants and passions. Somehow or other each group agreed on what to call certain things; *how* we do not know. There are various theories about the origins of language, but although they are very interesting, they remain speculative.

There is, however, one group of root words that forms an exception to this rule; we do know why they mean what they mean. These are the onomatopoeic words. This is a clumsy word for a very pretty concept. Onomatopoeic words are words that imitate natural sounds. They form an interesting and charming group. When we say that lions ROAR we are using a root word. We can clearly see that "roar" is an attempt to imitate the sound made by a lion. In the same way, bees buzz, snakes hiss, birds chirp, brooks babble, and so on.

But these onomatopoeic word roots are the exception; in all other cases, we do not know why the particular sequences of sounds were chosen to have the particular meanings assigned to them.

What the French Did to the Latin (and English) Language

In 1066, an event occurred that was destined to change the face of the English language forever. The French Duke of Normandy, known to all men as William the Conqueror, crossed the Channel and conquered England. With him came an army of Norman French soldiers, nobility, and officials. For the next three centuries, the Norman French and the Anglo-Saxon peoples and tongues lived side by side in England in a sort of uneasy truce.

Anglo-Saxon held its own strongly. The people stubbornly went on speaking it. Nevertheless, from the high echelons, there rained down into Anglo-Saxon a large number of French words. This was perhaps the greatest single infusion of a foreign language experienced by any language in modern times.

To appreciate the linguistic significance of this event, you must bear in mind something of unusual interest. When, in the first century B.C., Rome conquered France, the Gauls and later the Franks did bow in linguistic submission. They dropped their ancient Celtic and Germanic tongues and took over Latin as their spoken language. Being new to it, they were careless in speaking it. They softened, slurred and shortened words; hardly any Latin word escaped some mutilation. But even though words were changed, it is usually possible to see their Latin origins.

One of the commonest forms of the slurring of Latin words in the French was the dropping of the middle hard sound. For example, the French word for KINGLY became ROYAL, which was originally the Latin word REGAL with a hard "g" in the middle. Thus, when the Anglo-Saxons began to adopt French words, what they were really adopting were French versions of Latin words.

In the 1400's, the Renaissance occurred. This revival of interest in the ancient Greek and Latin cultures brought into English a vast number of Latin words directly from the Latin.

Now what frequently happened was this: English had already borrowed a certain French word; then during the days of the Renaissance, and almost continuously afterwards, English was borrowing directly from Latin. Frequently, English would borrow from the Latin the very same word that centuries before it had borrowed from the French. We therefore have a large number of what are called "doublets," two different words ultimately originating from the same source. Let us look at a few examples of this interesting series of words:

from the Latin	*from the French*
regal	royal
secure	sure
fragile	frail
decadence	decay
median (in the middle)	mean (average)
redemption (buying back)	ransom
senior	sire, sir
predatory	prey
tincture	taint

Another interesting and tricky change that French would often make in Latin words was to turn the hard "c" or "k" sound to a "ch." This changed the sound of the words sharply and often made them difficult to recognize. Very often these words, which the French had taken over from the Latin and then altered, were taken over in English; and the same words in their original Latin form were also taken over. These words now exist in English in two different forms:

1. The original Latin with the hard "c" or "k" sound.

2. With the "c" changed to the "ch" form of the French.

Here are some examples of these doublets:

from the Latin	*from the French*
trickery	treachery
cattle	chattel
canal	channel
cadence (the way things fall)	chance, chute, parachute
captain (the head man)	chief, achieve
incision (from "cis," *to cut*)	chisel
kirk	church

Word Roots and Affixes

So you see, when you begin to be able to recognize the roots of words, you can increase your vocabulary enormously. Words come in families, and the same root can be spotted in many different, but related, words. English borrowed from many other languages, and you will suddenly find that you know many foreign words.

Other languages also borrowed from English, especially in

science and technology. When you hear or see a foreign language many words will be familiar to you. It is fun to be a linguist, to figure out word meanings from their roots and changes.

In this book, we have identified as a word family all the words that have a common root or base. To this base may be added one or more prefixes (at the beginning of the root) or suffixes (at the end of the root). When this is done, the word is modified in some important way.

The meaning may be altered somewhat. For example, let us take the word ACT which means *to do* or *to perform*. Now, if we add the prefix "re," we have the word REACT, which means *to act in response to*. If we add the suffix "or" to the word ACT, we get ACTOR, or *a man who performs on the stage or in a movie*.

Adding prefixes or suffixes may change the meaning a great deal. For example, the word PRESS, meaning *to squeeze* or *to urge,* can become:

EXPRESS —— *to make known*
OPPRESS —— *to burden*
IMPRESS —— *to have an impact*
SUPPRESS —— *to squelch*
REPRESS —— *to hold back*
COMPRESS —— *to make compact*
DEPRESS —— *to sadden*

Some suffixes serve primarily to change the grammatical function of the word, rather than to alter its meaning substantially.

For example, if we add "ing" or "ed" to the word root ACT, we get ACTING and ACTED, with changes in tense only.

If we add "ion" to ACT or to REACT, we get ACTION or REACTION, and we have changed a verb into a noun.

Similarly, adding "ure" to PRESS changes the verb PRESS to a noun, PRESSURE; adding "ive" to IMPRESS gives IMPRESSIVE, forming an adjective from the verb.

When you become familiar with some of the basic prefixes and suffixes, you will readily see how they affect the meaning or grammatical function of the word root.

How New Words Are Coined

Language is a living, growing thing. It does not remain static, but keeps changing. Some words become obsolete and drop out of the language; some words change in meaning.

And new words are added all the time. Whenever a new invention or discovery is made, a new word must be coined. Sometimes the new word is simply the name of the inventor; for example, the word SANDWICH is said to have come from the Earl of Sandwich who is supposed to have created this type of food so that he would not have to leave the gambling table for meals.

Sometimes, the new word is borrowed from mythology; for example, the word VULCANIZE comes from the Roman god of fire and metal working, Vulcan.

Sometimes, the new word is made up of the first letters of the phrase that explains the new word; for example, RADAR comes from *ra*dio *d*etecting *a*nd *r*anging.

The word JEEP uses initials plus an onomatopoeic device. This *G*eneral *P*urpose car, developed for the U.S. Army in World War II, is supposedly named after the sound made by a funny little animal character, Eugene the Jeep, invented by the comic strip cartoonist E.C. Segar.

Sometimes, the new word is made from a foreign root. One such interesting word is ANESTHESIA.

Anesthesia was first used by Dr. William T.S. Morton in 1846, at the Massachusetts General Hospital. Bending over his patient, a 20-year old man with a tumor on his jaw, the doctor asked:

"Are you ready for the operation?"

"Yes" came the weak answer.

The spectators burst into laughter and cheers. *The operation had already been performed.* Dr. Morton had discovered that ether caused insensibility to pain, and he had had the patient breathe in ether just before the operation. For the first time in human history, the knife cut living flesh and there was no pain.

It was one of the great moments in time. A world weary with pain at once recognized the triumph, and rejoiced. Oliver Wendell Holmes, Sr., the great American writer and physician, rose to the occasion and added two words to the English language. Using the Greek root "aisthesis," for *feeling* or *sensation,* he added the prefix "an," meaning *without* and coined the word ANESTHESIA, *loss of the sense of pain,* and the word ANESTHETIC, *the drug that causes anesthesia.* An ANESTHETIST or ANESTHESIOLOGIST is a *doctor specializing in administering anesthetics.*

The word ESTHETE, meaning a *person with an exaggerated feeling for art and beauty,* is also related to the Greek root "aisthesis," as is the word ESTHETIC, for *artistic.*

So, here is WORDS COME IN FAMILIES. I hope it provides pleasurable instruction.

E.H.

ALLOS ALTER

Meaning: Other.

Origin: Latin, *alter,* other.
            Greek, *allos,* other.

Man, being basically gregarious by nature, likes to live in the company of groups of people who are like himself. He feels threatened by people and things other than those he is used to.

Most of the words that derive from the root meaning *other* seem to have negative undertones. The one remarkable exception—the word ALTRUISM—means *unselfishness.*

An ALIEN, a person who comes from another land, is often regarded with suspicion because he is a stranger. The Bible, recognizing the loneliness and vulnerability of the alien, insists on understanding and justice for the stranger.

You shall love the alien, the stranger, because you were aliens in the land of Egypt.

There shall be but one law for you and for the alien who lives in your midst.

ALTRUISM

Concern for the welfare of others, acting in an unselfish way to help others.

When the earthquake struck, people from all over the world, out of a sense of altruism, volunteered their help to the victims.

ALIEN

Belonging to another country, a foreigner, an outsider; strange to, not natural.

To the alien who was trying to learn English, it was alien to protrude his tongue in order to pronounce "th."

ALLERGY

Reaction in a way other than usual; sensitiveness to certain foods, animals, pollen, etc.

After being in the room with the cat for five minutes, her allergy began to act up and she started to sneeze.

ALTER

To make different, to change.

When she lost weight, she had to have all her clothes altered to fit her new size.

ALTERNATIVE

Another possibility, another choice.

John's parents could no longer pay for his college fees, and he had no alternative but to find a job.

ALTER EGO

Another self; a very close friend.

Dr. Jekyll and Mr. Hyde were alter egos in a tale of horror.

ALIAS

Another name; an assumed name.

To keep the police off his tracks, he assumed an alias every time he moved.

ALTERNATE

To follow one thing with another; to take turns.

John alternated with Jim in taking the night shift on alternate weeks.

ALLEGORY

A story in which the people, the objects, and the events are symbols that have other meanings.

George Orwell's Animal Farm *is an allegory in which animals behave like people.*

A M B U L

Meaning: To walk, to move.

Origin: Latin, *ambulare*, to walk, to go.

It is a bit puzzling. How do we get from "ambul" which is clearly related to the action of walking, to the AMBULANCE wildly chasing down the street to administer emergency medical care?

The explanation is clear: In days of old, soldiers wounded on the field of battle were just left there to suffer or to die. But in the mid-nineteenth century, the French developed an *hôpital ambulant*. This was simply a mobile hospital whose personnel went forth to the wounded soldier to try to save his life.

As is the way with language, words or phrases that are too long and cumbersome get shortened. In this case, the "hospital" part was dropped and only the "ambulant" part remained. This became our English word ambulance, which still retains the idea of hospital service.

Later, when the automobile was invented, the ambulance no longer went; it sped.

AMBULATORY

Able to walk.

After being confined to his bed for so long, the patient was thrilled to be able to get out of bed and become ambulatory.

PREAMBLE

That which goes before, an introductory statement.

The preamble to the American Constitution expresses a dedication to the cause of freedom and justice.

AMBLE

To walk in a leisurely manner; to move at an easy pace.

With their arms around each other's waist, the lovers slowly ambled down the street.

AMBULANCE

A special vehicle for transporting the sick or wounded.

The boy who was hurt in the accident was rushed to the hospital in an ambulance.

PERAMBULATOR

A carriage for taking a baby outdoors.

In England, a baby carriage or buggy is called a "pram," short for "perambulator."

SOMNAMBULIST

A sleepwalker.

Just as the somnambulist reached the top of the stairs, his mother shrieked, and luckily, he woke up.

ARCH

Meaning: Beginning; the first, the leader, the ruler.

Origin: Greek, *arch*, beginning, ruler.

In every primary school, whenever children line up, each child clamors to be first on line. Children deem first an advantageous position. In many cultures being the first-born holds many privileges, both legal and traditional.

The family of words with the common root "arch" seems to contain words that are very different from each other. But they all have something in common: they are all related to the concept of *first*.

Being first has two different, but often related, meanings: one meaning indicates *first in time;* another indicates *first in importance*.

MONARCH

The sole ruler of a state.

Louis XVI, the monarch of France, was beheaded during the French Revolution.

ARCHBISHOP

The chief bishop of a diocese.

Thomas Becket, the archbishop of Canterbury, was murdered when he opposed King Henry II.

ARCHITECT

The chief builder or designer.

The Guggenheim Museum in New York City was designed by the famous American architect Frank Lloyd Wright.

PATRIARCH

The father or ruler of a family or group.

Abraham was a Biblical patriarch who is said to be the founder of the Hebrew tribe.

MATRIARCH

The mother or woman who rules the family or tribe.

The 70-year-old grandmother was the matriarch of the family.

ARCHEOLOGY, ARCHEOLOGIST

The study of ancient civilizations; a scientist who excavates ancient cities.

We have learned much about the age and origin of man from bones excavated by archeologists.

ARCHDIOCESE

The district presided over by an archbishop.

The archdiocese of New York is proud of Mother Seton, a New Yorker who was declared to be the first American saint.

HIERARCHY

A group arranged in order of rank or grade.

The President is at the head of the governmental hierarchy.

ANARCHY

Without a leader; absence of government and law.

After the revolution, there was complete anarchy in the land.

ARCHDUKE

A chief duke.

The assassination of Archduke Francis Ferdinand of Austria on June 28, 1914 precipitated World War I.

ARCHETYPE

Chief model.

Satan is the archetype of evil.

ARCHIPELAGO

A sea with a cluster of islands.

The Aegean archipelago lies between Greece and Turkey.

ARCHAIC

Belonging to ancient times; old-fashioned.

The word "thou" is an archaic form of "you."

ARCHENEMY

Chief enemy.

Disease is the archenemy of mankind.

ARCHANGEL

Chief angel.

Gabriel was one of the seven archangels.

BELL

Meaning: War.

Origin: Latin, *bellum,* war.
Latin, *bellare,* to wage war.

So momentous an event in American history was the Civil War, that Latin nomenclature is retained to endow it with appropriate dignity: ANTEBELLUM characterizes the period before the advent of the Civil War, while POSTBELLUM refers to the post-Civil War years.

War rarely resolves problems. Many wars have been fought in this world, and much blood has been shed—almost always to no avail. A famous Latin phrase describes this situation: *status quo ante bellum* means that after a war things remain just the same as before.

REBEL

A person who resists or opposes authority; to revolt.

The American policy in Viet Nam created many rebels on America's college campuses.

BELLICOSE

Inclined to fighting, hostile, quarrelsome.

His puny size and build would have made him a natural target for teasing, but his bellicose manner deterred others from bullying him.

BELLIGERENT

Engaged in war; a person, group, or nation provoking or engaging in battle.

The Arab nations refused to approve a non-belligerency clause in any agreement with Israel.

CAD   CAS   CID

Meaning: To fall.

Origin: Latin, *cadere,* to fall.

Why should the word OCCIDENT, which means *the lands of the West,* be based on a root which means *to fall?*

The answer is rather simple. To ancient people, the rising of the sun each morning was a dramatic event, signalling the end of night and the beginning of day.

When the sun went down at the end of the day, it was seen to fall in the general direction of the Western lands. All ancient people reckoned their directions by the rising and setting of the sun. The Orient meant the direction of the rising sun, the lands of the East.

Today, when you orient yourself, you determine your position. You may or may not use the sun as your guide, but your ancestors certainly did.

ACCIDENT

A sudden fall or collision; an unexpected happening.

A three-car accident tied up the highway traffic for hours.

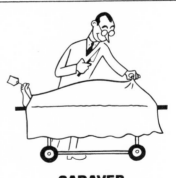

CADAVER

A fallen or dead body; a corpse.

The doctor performed an autopsy on the cadaver to determine the cause of death.

OCCASION

A happening; a special event.

He was filled with both joy and fear on the occasion of his wedding.

OCCASIONAL

Happening now and then; infrequent.

My 90-year-old aunt claims that an occasional drink keeps her young.

CADENZA

A brilliant musical passage, rich in rises and falls.

At the end of the first movement of the concerto, there was a beautifully played cadenza for the flute.

COINCIDE

To be exactly the same; to occur at the same time.

They get along very well because their interests coincide.

DECADENCE

A falling or decline in morals or culture.

During its decline, the Roman Empire was noted for its decadence.

DECIDUOUS

Falling off at certain seasons or stages of growth; short lived; temporary.

Deciduous trees shed their leaves every fall.

COINCIDENCE, COINCIDENT

Falling together.

It was just by coincidence that the two ladies wore the same dress to the party.

CADENCE

The rise and fall of the voice in talking; rhythmic movement in dancing or marching.

Sometimes it is possible to recognize which foreign language is being spoken just by listening to the cadence.

CASE

An example or occurrence; something that happened to befall.

Parents were asked to examine their children carefully because there were three cases of chicken pox in the school.

OCCIDENT

Direction of the setting (falling) sun; the Western hemisphere.

Some historians are predicting that in the near future there will be a shift of power from the Occident to the Orient.

INCIDENT

An occurrence; something that befell; a minor event.

Falling on his head was just one of the minor incidents in John's traumatic first five years of life.

CHANCE

A happening; an accidental occurrence.

The two friends met by chance on their vacation.

DECAY

To lose strength; to deteriorate, waste away.

If you do not take good care of your teeth, they may decay.

C A N D

Meaning: To glow, to be shining white, to burn.

Origin: Latin, *candere,* to glow white.

With political corruption making daily headlines, and with elected officials serving jail terms, we can't help but marvel at the fact that the word CANDIDATE derives from the root which means *to be shining white*. White, of course, symbolizes purity.

The meaning of the root originated with an old Roman custom. When a man ran for public office in ancient Rome, he bought himself a toga—a long, shining, white cloak. With this garb, the candidate stood out in a crowd. The people took notice of him and, because of his white garment, associated the candidate with purity and goodness.

CANDELABRUM

A large, branched candlestick.

The beautiful silver candelabrum sat on the shelf and was only taken down to be used for very special occasions.

CANDLE

A cylinder of wax with a wick enclosed which gives light when burned.

Before the days of gas and electricity, candles were the main source of light.

INCENSE

Spices burnt for their sweet smell.

In temples throughout the world, priests often burn incense as part of the religious service.

INCENSE

To make someone burn with anger.

The teacher was incensed at the unruly behavior of the pupil.

CANDOR

Honesty, frankness, sincerity, freedom from bias.

Alice admired John's candor in talking about what went wrong with his first marriage.

CHANDELIER

A branched lighting fixture, usually hanging from the ceiling.

The crystal chandelier spread a cheerful glow in the elegant dining room.

INCANDESCENT

Very bright, glowing with light or heat.

In 1879, Thomas Alva Edison invented the incandescent electric bulb.

INCENDIARY

A person who deliberately starts a fire; stirring up trouble.

His speech in defense of abortion was highly incendiary to his mostly Catholic audience.

CANDID

Honest, frank, outspoken, unbiased.

Mary decided to be candid with Paul and told him she liked him but was not in love with him.

CANDIDATE

A person who seeks to run for an office.

The conservative candidate promised to eliminate inflation, and the liberal candidate promised to eliminate unemployment.

CANEH

Meaning: Reed, tube.

Origin: Hebrew, *kaneh,* reed.
Latin, *canna,* reed, pipe.

Long ago, tall, slender, and hollow reeds grew on the banks of the Jordan and the Nile Rivers. The word for reed in the Hebrew, Arabic, and Egyptian languages was *kaneh.* The word passed over into Greek and Latin, and into the languages of western Europe.

A rather remarkable word family grew from the root "canna." Some are easy to trace back. Sugar CANE, a walking CANE, even a CANNON are all clearly related to the reed in shape. With just a little imagination, the words CANAL and CHANNEL can also be associated with a pipe or groove.

But it is a bit more difficult to see how the word CANON, or *law,* derives from the root meaning *reed.* Since reeds were long and straight, they were often used as measuring rods. And so the word REED came to mean *a standard;* ultimately, *an authoritative standard,* or *law.*

CANONIZE

To declare someone a saint.

Five hundred years after she was burned at the stake for witchcraft, Joan of Arc was canonized.

CANAL

A groove; an artificial waterway.

The Panama Canal connects the Atlantic and Pacific Oceans.

CANYON

A narrow valley between high cliffs.

The Indians used smoke signals to communicate across canyons.

CANNON

A large gun.

The roar of the cannon announced that the parade had begun.

CANE

A walking stick.

The old man beat off the robber with his cane.

A plant with a slender, hollow stem.

Sugar went up in price because the sugar cane crop was poor.

CANISTER

A can for storing things.

The canister was labeled "sugar," but when he used some of the powder in his coffee he realized it was salt.

CHANNEL

A long groove; a body of water joining two larger bodies of water; a passageway.

The English Channel is an arm of the Atlantic Ocean separating England and France.

A transmitting band assigned to a broadcast station.

Channel 13 has many educational television programs.

To direct into a groove.

To achieve a goal, you have to channel your energies in one direction.

CANON

A law; a criterion or standard used in judging.

A recent Church canon liberalized the religious prohibition against eating meat on Friday.

CAP   CEPT

Meaning: To take, to seize.

Origin: Latin, *capere,* to take.

This word root forms a small, but important, part of a large and important word: EMANCIPATION. When you become experienced at finding roots, prefixes, and suffixes in words, you will be able to take long words apart, and then put the parts together to discover the meaning of the word. Let us do that with the word EMANCIPATION:

E is short for "ex," and means *out of*

MAN, short for "manus," means *hand*

CIP is the root *to take*

TION is a suffix which is used to make a noun from a verb.

Thus, emancipation means *the act of taking out of the hand,* hence, the act of setting free.

On January 1, 1863, President Abraham Lincoln issued the Emancipation Proclamation, which declared that all slaves were free.

CONCEIVE

To take in; to understand, apprehend, imagine; to become pregnant.

I can't conceive that a woman of 90 should conceive, but the Bible says that Sarah gave birth to Isaac when she was 90.

INTERCEPT

To take, seize, or stop on the way; to interrupt, hinder, prevent.

The secret war message was intercepted and decoded, removing the element of surprise from the attack.

CAPABLE

Able to take hold; skilled, competent.

He was capable of lifting 500 lbs. with no sweat.

RECEIVE

To get, to acquire, to take into one's possession.

Louise received many birthday gifts.

ACCEPT

To take willingly.

John was thrilled that Mary accepted his proposal of marriage.

CAPACIOUS

Able to hold a lot, roomy, spacious.

He likes a jacket with capacious pockets so he can stuff a lot of things into them.

CAPTURE

To take by force or surprise, to seize.

The police captured the bank robbers just as they were about to make their getaway.

CAPTURE

To grasp the essence.

With a few strokes of his brush, the artist captured the man's personality in his portrait.

EXCEPT

Taking or leaving out, omitting, excluding.

All the children got balloons, except Mark, who got a kite.

CAPTIVE

A person held in confinement, a prisoner.

The natives held him captive while they performed their war dance.

CAPTIVATE

To take with one's charms, to hold the attention or affection, to fascinate.

The opera singer captivated the audience with her looks, voice, and dramatic flair.

PERCEPTION

Taking in through the senses or the mind, awareness, insight, intuition.

The mother's perception of her son's needs was different from her husband's.

PRECEPT

A rule of action or moral conduct.

Some people act in accordance with the precept that the end justifies the means.

EMANCIPATE

To set free.

The Women's Lib(eration) movement would like to emancipate women from their "place in the home."

PARTICIPATE

To take part in, to share in.

Every pupil in the class participated in the performance.

SUSCEPTIBLE

Able to take in; sensitive; responsive; easily affected or influenced.

The infant was highly susceptible to colds.

ANTICIPATE

To feel beforehand, to expect, to look forward to.

Anticipating that a shortage would cause a rise in price, they stocked up on sugar.

DECEIVE

To take the truth from a person, to delude, to mislead.

He deceived his mother into believing he was going to school when he really went to the movies.

CONCEIT

Taking in an exaggerated self-concept, vanity, holding a high opinion of one's own merits.

Since he won the race, he has been full of conceit about his athletic prowess.

CAPACITY

The ability to contain or hold.

The capacity of the elevator was 1500 lbs.

Aptitude.

He has the capacity to learn, but he is lazy and doesn't try.

CAPIT CHIEF

Meaning: Head, chief.

Origin: Latin, *caput,* head.
          French, *chef,* head, chief.

You might be surprised to see that a CAPTAIN and a CHEF both belong to the same word family. A captain is, of course, *the head of a company of soldiers,* and a chef is *the captain of the cooks.* A chef, especially to all of us who love good food, is not a lowly official. And, when you remember the old saying that an army travels on its stomach, a chef is every bit as important as a captain.

The linguistic relationship between these two words manifests a rule we talked about earlier in this book. When the French borrowed words from the Latin, they frequently softened the sounds. These French words, with their softer sounds, then made their way into the English language. At the same time, English borrowed words directly from Latin. Thus, in English we often have two words which share the same root, but which have different (though related) forms and meanings.

Here are some more examples of pairs of words that retain the *k* sound of the Latin and the *ch* sound of the French:

Latin form		*French form*	
BLANK	= empty	BLANCH	= to make white
BANK	= an establishment for receiving, keeping, lending money	BENCH	= a long seat; originally the money-changers conducted business on benches.

CASTLE = massive strong-hold of noblemen in Middle Ages

CHATEAU = a large country house or castle

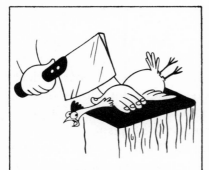

DECAPITATE

To cut off the head.

With one swift blow, the butcher decapitated the chicken.

KERCHIEF

A piece of cloth worn on the head or around the neck.

The girl's long golden hair hung down below her kerchief.

CHAPTER

A main heading or division of a book; a local branch of a club or organization.

At their last meeting, the Rockland chapter of the Bible Study Association read and discussed Chapter VII of Genesis.

PRECIPICE

A steep cliff; a place from which you can fall headlong; a dangerous situation.

On his graduation day, John felt as though he were at the edge of a precipice.

CAPTAIN

An army officer.

The captain ordered his men to fire.

CAPTAIN

The leader of a sports team.

The captain of the football team gave his men their signals.

CHEF

A head cook.

The chef made a roast fit for a king.

PRECIPITATION

A headlong rush of water or chemicals; the amount of rain, snow, sleet.

When the weather forecast predicts a high precipitation level, you can expect rain.

MISCHIEF

Coming to a bad or wrong end; a prank, a playful annoying act.

On Halloween, look out for mischief makers.

CHIEF

The head person; the main thing.

One of the chief causes of crime is poverty.

PRECIPITATE

Throw headlong; to bring on suddenly, hastily or unexpectedly.

The steep rise in prices precipitated street rioting.

CAPITULATE

To give up, to stop resisting, to surrender.

When the government called out the troops, the strikers capitulated and went back to their jobs.

ACHIEVE

To bring to a head; to accomplish; to do successfully.

To achieve what you want in life, it helps to be a little lucky.

RECAPITULATE

To summarize the chief ideas; to repeat briefly.

When the professor had finished his lecture, the secretary recapitulated the talk in a few words.

CAPITAL

A chief city.

Paris is the capital of France.

A letter of the alphabet larger than its corresponding small letter.

A capital letter is always used at the beginning of a sentence.

Accumulated wealth.

The fifty cents in my pocket is all the capital I have.

CAPS

Meaning: Container; box.

Origin: Latin, *capsa,* a box, a chest.
French, *casse,* a case.

As words made their way from one language into another, their pronunciation was somewhat altered. Sometimes letters were dropped, while other times letters were added or changed.

This, in turn, led to alterations in meaning. Thus, there are many words which, on the surface, do not seem to be related, but which actually stem from the same root.

When the Latin word "capsa" entered French, the *p* was dropped. The resultant "casse" later became the English word CASE (*container*) as in WATCHCASE.

This should not be confused with "case" in the sense of a legal case. The legal case came from the Latin word "casus," which derived from "cadere," *to fall.* Thus the English word CASE has two different meanings, and two different origins.

CAPSULE

A small soluble gelatin container within which is a dose of medicine.

The doctor prescribed three capsules of aureomycin a day.

CASSETTE

A plastic box for recorded tapes.

Many people keep cassette recorders in their cars.

CASKET

A coffin.

He was buried in a simple wooden casket.

CASE

A box or crate.

He brought a case of beer to the party.

CASH

Money on hand, bills and coins (originally kept in a box).

They would not accept his check, so he was obliged to pay in cash.

CEDE   CEED   CESS

Meaning: To go, to go away, to yield.

Origin: Latin, *cedere,* to go, to yield.

From the primitive baying of the hound, to the complicated signal system of the bee, all members of the animal kingdom employ some means of communication. But only man developed the arbitrary system of symbols called language.

Language is a marvelous mechanism. Words, the tools of language, can express differences in meaning from the infinite to the infinitesimal.

It is easy to see how the meaning is changed when we add familiar suffixes to familiar roots, as in: big, bigger, biggest; care, careful, careless. Just a bit more experience and imagination is necessary to track down more subtle changes with less familiar roots.

Take the root "cede," for example, which means *to go.* It is easy to see that PROCEED means *to go forward,* and RECEDE means *to go back.* Nor is it so hard to guess that CONCEDE means *to go along with,* or *to give in to;* and that ACCEDE means *to go along with,* or *to agree.*

When you go away from what you were doing, you CEASE or *stop;* until finally, you go away forever when you are DECEASED, or *dead.*

A most interesting word family.

CEASE

To stop; to end; to discontinue; to withdraw.

The fighting did not cease even though the truce was signed.

PROCEED

To go on.

They tried to proceed with their meeting after it had been interrupted by the bomb scare.

ACCESS

Way to go in or enter,
approach, admittance.

*There was a long line of cars
waiting for access to the
tunnel.*

ACCEDE

To give in; to assent; to agree.

*The henpecked husband ac-
ceded to every demand made
by his domineering wife.*

EXCEED

To go beyond; to be more
than; to surpass; to outdo.

*The police officer gave him a
ticket for exceeding the speed
limit.*

PROCESSION

A line of people going in an
orderly fashion; a marching
together.

*The soldiers moved in a stately
procession before the king.*

RECEDE

To go or move back; to withdraw.

He was very worried about his receding hairline.

DECEASE

To go away; to die; death.

He had warm and tender memories of his deceased wife.

CONCESSION

Something granted or yielded; the right to run a food or newspaper, etc. stall.

In order to be sure of at least one meal a day, the aspiring actress worked in the hat check concession of a restaurant.

SECEDE

To go out; to withdraw formally from membership in a group.

The Civil War resulted from the South's desire to secede from the Union.

ANTECEDENT

Going before.

The antecedent to a pronoun is generally a noun.

Preceding.

Events antecedent to the surprise attack had not aroused anyone's suspicions.

ANCESTOR

A person who came before; a forebear from whom one in descended.

Some people find it hard to believe that the ape is man's ancestor.

ACCESSORY

Someone or something that goes along with; some extra equipment.

The car was a deluxe model with many accessories such as power windows, stereo tape deck, etc.

Helping in an unlawful act.

He helped to hide the escaped robber and thus was held as an accessory to the crime.

RECESSION

Going backward; a temporary falling off of business activity.

The rising rate of unemployment makes everyone wonder whether the recession is really a depression.

CONCEDE

To yield in an argument; to admit the truth or justice of; to acknowledge.

The strike ended when the employer conceded to the demands of the workers.

PRECEDENT

An act or case or decision that goes first and serves as a rule, pattern, or justification for a later act.

They would not allow the mother to bring her baby to the meeting because that would establish a poor precedent; they might then be flooded with children at all their meetings.

INACCESSIBLE

Impossible to reach or enter, inapproachable, unobtainable.

The ball had rolled under a car and was inaccessible.

PRECEDE

To go before.

The debate turned into an endless discussion of which precedes which: the chicken or the egg.

PROCESS

A method or course of doing something.

The alchemists tried to invent a process for making gold from base metals.

CERN CERT

Meaning: To perceive, to separate, to distinguish.

Origin: Latin, *cernere,* to decide, to separate
Latin, *certus,* certain, fixed.

You might wonder why these two roots have been put together. "Certus" is the past participle of "cernere." The root "cern" means *to sift material (such as flour) through a sieve,* or in other words, *to separate a mass into several parts.* All the words in this family have something to do with recognizing or perceiving known parts.

CERTIFICATE

A document formally attesting to a fact, qualification or status.

The young doctor had all his certificates framed on his wall.

DISCERN

To recognize the difference, to make out clearly, to perceive.

Even their own mother could not discern any difference between the identical twins.

ASCERTAIN

To find out for sure, to make certain.

Before he hired her, he checked her references to ascertain her qualifications.

CONCERN

To relate to, to affect, to interest; worry or anxiety; a business company or firm.

She led her own life and was not at all concerned about her husband's concern.

CERTIFY

To formally declare something true, accurate, certain.

The doctor certified that the criminal was insane.

CERTAIN

Settled, sure; some.

Although the doctor believed that the pill was certain to prevent colds, in certain cases it did not work.

INDISCRIMINATE

Making no distinctions, confused.

The old woman was indiscriminate in her charity and gave to all who begged, regardless of need or merit.

DISCRIMINATE

To see differences between.

He does not drive because he is color blind and cannot discriminate between red and green.

To distinguish unfavorably against.

When he failed to get the job, he said he had been discriminated against because of his religion.

DISCREET

Careful about what one says or does, prudent.

He noticed that she was wearing two different shoes, but he was too discreet to call that to her attention.

CHRON

Meaning: Time.

Origin: Greek, *chron,* time.

Herodotus, who lived in the 5th Century B.C., wrote the story or CHRONICLE of the wars between the Greeks and the Persians. For this reason, Herodotus has been considered as the "Father of History."

Actually, the books of Samuel in the Bible antedate Herodotus by several centuries. These biblical chronicles relate the stories of King Saul and King David.

CHRONOMETER

A highly accurate instrument for measuring time precisely.

A chronometer is used to determine a ship's longitude at sea.

ANACHRONISM

Out of its proper historical time; showing something as existing earlier than it did.

The picture of Julius Caesar reading by lamplight contains a glaring anachronism.

SYNCHRONIZE

To occur at the same time, to be simultaneous.

It was very annoying to watch the movie because the sound track was not synchronized with the action.

CHRONICLE

A narrative history, a record of facts or events in order of time.

Gone with the Wind *is a chronicle of a Southern family during the Civil War.*

CHRONOLOGICAL

Arranged in order of time of occurrence.

The history test listed a series of events which the students had to put in chronological order.

CHRONIC

Lasting a long time; recurrent, habitual.

Arthritis is a chronic disease.

CIDE   CIS

Meaning: To cut; to kill.

Origin: Latin, *cidia, caedere,* to cut down, to strike mortally.

The world's first murder was a FRATRICIDE. The story is recorded in the Bible.

Two brothers had a quarrel. Cain rose up against his brother Abel and slew him. The murderer fled from the wrath of the Lord and hid in the deep thickets of the forest where the light of the sun never penetrated. And there, in the dark and the stillness, the voice of God came to him, searching, testing, inquiring:

"Where is your brother Abel?"

Back came Cain's lying, contemptuous answer:

"Am I my brother's keeper?"

And the Lord God said:

"What have you done? Your brother's blood cries out to me from the ground."

Thus the first murder established the first moral precept: Every man *is* his brother's keeper, responsible for his brother's fate and his welfare.

SUICIDE

Killing oneself.

About 1,000 people commit suicide every day throughout the world.

Action destructive to one's interests or career.

It would be political suicide for a senator from Texas to oppose the oil industry.

HOMICIDE

The killing of a human being, murder, manslaughter.

In some states, homicide is punishable by death.

INCISOR

A front tooth.

We use our incisors for biting food.

DECIDE

To cut through doubts or problems, to settle, to pass judgment.

She couldn't decide which of the two dresses to buy, so she tossed a coin.

CHISEL

A tool for cutting wood, stone or metal.

The sculptor used a chisel to obtain precise features.

INSECTICIDE

A substance used to kill insects.

She used an insecticide against the roaches that had infested her kitchen.

GENOCIDE

The systematic killing or extermination of a people.

Hitler's attempted genocide of the Jews resulted in six million dead.

CIRCUMCISE

To cut off part of the foreskin in a religious rite.

Jews and Mohammedans circumcise their male young.

INCISIVE

Cutting into, penetrating.

The book was heavily researched and presented a clear and incisive analysis of the events leading up to the war.

CONCISE

Cutting off all extras; brief and to the point.

The speaker was allotted a few minutes for his talk, so he had to be concise.

FRATRICIDE

Killing one's own brother or sister.

The first recorded murder was the fratricide of Abel by his brother Cain.

PRECISE

Cut short, exact, definite, with no variation.

Our English teacher demands precise observance of the rules of grammar.

INCISION

Cutting into something; a cut or gash.

The surgeon made a quick, clean incision into the man's stomach.

C I T

Meaning: To summon, to put into motion, to impel.

Origin: Latin, *citare,* to arouse, to summon, to set moving.

In the course of time, a word sometimes undergoes changes in meaning. As it is used in different contexts, a word may take on different connotations—sometimes positive, sometimes negative. The word NICE, for example, originally meant *not knowing,* hence, *ignorant* or *foolish.* Then it came to mean: *difficult to please, picky,* having high standards. Now, NICE has become a watered down, innocuous word meaning *pleasant* or *agreeable.*

The word KNAVE seems to have followed the opposite course. Coming from the German "knabe," it originally meant *male child* or *boy.* It was then used to indicate a *male servant* or *serving boy.* Since this position was generally held by poor boys of low status, KNAVE soon began to suggest *a dishonest, tricky person,* or *a rascal.*

The word SILLY also did a turn for the worse. Beginning by meaning *blessed* or *happy,* the meaning of the word changed gradually into *innocent,* or *unworldly,* and finally reached its current meaning of *foolish* or *stupid.*

A word that is beginning to take on pejorative connotations in our time is INCITE. Its literal meaning is neutral: to *stimulate* or to *urge to action.* But in recent history, the word has often been used in connection with activities of demagogues or rabble rousers. For example, we speak of McCarthy *inciting* Americans to Red-baiting, and of Hitler and Stalin *inciting* religious and political persecution. Today, we tend to associate the word INCITE with the stirring up of evil impulses and deeds.

CITATION

Quotation; honorable mention.

The fireman received a citation for his bravery in rescuing the people from the burning building.

RECITE

To repeat aloud from memory.

The audience shifted restlessly in their seats while the child recited "The Charge of the Light Brigade."

INCITE

To stimulate; to urge to action.

The new law raising taxes incited protest from both rich and poor.

EXCITED

Stirred up; aroused.

Everybody became very excited when a shark was spotted in the water.

RESUSCITATE

To bring back to life, to revive.

They rescued the drowning boy and resuscitated him through mouth-to-mouth breathing.

CITE

To quote; to refer to as proof, example, or explanation.

To support his view on conservation, the speaker cited the arguments of experts in the field of ecology.

CLAM

Meaning: To call out.

Origin: Latin, *clamare,* to cry out.

Today, it is easy to find out what events are occurring around the world. One simply has to turn on the radio or television news or read a newspaper or news magazine. But did you ever wonder how news spread before all these modern means of communication existed?

In days of old, all public announcements were actually called out by the town crier. PROCLAMATION, *a calling forth,* was the only means of spreading news or announcing a new law.

ACCLAIM

To shout approval, to applaud enthusiastically.

The audience acclaimed the ballet dancer's performance with flowers and applause.

CLAMOR

A loud outcry, noisy demand or complaint; confused noise.

The students greeted the teacher's announcement of a test with a clamor of protest and outrage.

CLAIM

To demand as one's right; to assert, to state as a fact.

John and George each claimed that the baseball bat was his.

DECLAIM

To speak loudly, to give a recitation, to deliver an impassioned speech.

The priest declaimed the funeral oration in loud and moving tones.

PROCLAIM

To announce officially, to declare publicly.

After winning every competition, he was proclaimed "campus athlete of the year."

EXCLAIM

To cry out, to speak vehemently as in surprise, anger or pain.

When his wife announced she was leaving him, he exclaimed, "After all I've done for you!"

RECLAIM

To ask for the return of, to try to get back.

Upon the presentation of proper identification, lost property can be reclaimed at the Lost and Found.

PROCLAMATION

An official announcement.

President Lincoln issued the Emancipation Proclamation to free the slaves.

CLAIMANT

A person who makes a claim.

The claimant told the jury that she had fallen down a flight of stairs because the landlord had neglected to repair a broken step.

DISCLAIM

To maintain you have no connection with a given thing, to deny, to repudiate.

Despite the testimony of the eyewitness, the driver of the car disclaimed any responsibility for the accident.

CLUD CLUS CLAUS

Meaning: To close, to shut.

Origin: Latin *claudere,* to shut, to block up.

There is a tendency in human nature (which is even reflected in the words we use) to *like* those who are *like* ourselves, and to be *kind* to those who are our *kind.*

Conversely, we tend to EXCLUDE people who are different from us.

Why do we shut them out? Psychologists say the reason is that such people pose a threat to us. If, by excluding them, we can make them feel inferior, then by the same token, we can feel EXCLUSIVE, or superior.

Wouldn't it be a fine thing for mankind if we followed Edwin Markham's poem:

> *He drew a circle that shut me out —*
> *Heretic, rebel, a thing to flout.*
> *But Love and I had the wit to win:*
> *We drew a circle that took him in!*

ENCLOSE

To shut in, to fence in.

The sheep were enclosed in the meadow.

To insert in an envelope.

Please enclose the bill along with your check.

OCCLUDE

To stop up, to block passage, to shut in or out.

A malfunction of the locks will sometimes occlude a canal, and ships will have to take an alternate route.

CLAUSTROPHOBIA

Fear of enclosed or confined places.

The New York City subway during rush hour is no place for a person with claustrophobia.

CLOSET

A small enclosure, a small room for clothes or household goods.

Our dog likes to hide in the closet.

CLAUSE

A group of words enclosed within a sentence; an article in a legal document.

Many research reports contain the clause "other things being equal."

EXCLUSIVE

Closed off to certain people or groups, snobbish or un-democratic, not shared.

Madam Renée runs an exclusive beauty shop that has exclusive rights to certain cosmetics.

RECLUSE

A person who is shut away from the world.

After his wife died, he shut himself up in his house and became a recluse.

INCLUDE

To contain within as part of a whole.

The restaurant bill included taxes and tips.

PRECLUDE

To shut out, to prevent, to make impossible, to hinder in advance.

Accepting the appointment with the Government precluded him from practicing privately.

SECLUDE

To shut off from others, to keep away from company, to isolate.

When they wanted to be alone, they met in a secluded spot far out of town.

CLOSE

To shut; near.

We keep the windows open all spring and fall, but when it gets close to winter we have to close the windows.

To complete, settle.

They put their house up for sale in July, and one month later they closed the deal.

CONCLUDE

To bring to a close, to come to an end, to settle; to decide.

Their dispute was quickly concluded, once both parties concluded that it would be better to settle out of court.

DISCLOSE

To bring into the open, to make known, to reveal.

After she had promised to forgive him, he disclosed that he was really guilty.

EXCLUDE

To shut out, to bar, to keep from entering.

Some country clubs still exclude Jews and Blacks from membership in disregard of the law.

CRAT

Meaning: To rule.

Origin: Greek, *kratein*, *kratos*, to rule, power.

Louis the XIV of France proclaimed, "I am the State." King James of England stated, "Kings have a divine right to rule."

These rulers were asserting the belief that government should be an AUTOCRACY, with supreme power in the hands of one ruler.

With the American and the French Revolutions, there arose the idea of DEMOCRACY. In a democracy, governmental power resides with the people.

AUTOCRACY

Absolute power, a government ruled by one individual with supreme power; dictatorship despotism.

Some families resemble autocracies, with the father making all the decisions for every family member.

DEMOCRACY

Government by the people or by their elected representatives, rule by majority; equality of rights.

The teacher ran his classroom like a democracy, with students free to express their ideas and desires.

ARISTOCRACY

Government by a privileged minority, or by a wealthy upper class or nobility.

The Russian Revolution took power away from the aristocracy and transferred authority to the Communist Party.

PLUTOCRACY

Rule by the wealthy.

The revolutionary movement aimed to overthrow the plutocracy that ruled the country.

ARISTOCRAT

A member of the upper or ruling class; a person with the tastes or manners of the nobility.

Though she no longer had wealth or power, the Countess had the bearing of an aristocrat.

One of the elite.

Champagne is the aristocrat of wines.

CRED

Meaning: To believe.

Origin: Latin, *credere*, to trust, believe.

The Latin word "credo" means *I believe*. When this word was absorbed into English, it became a noun meaning *a man's belief as to how he should carry on his life*.

From time immemorial, people have wondered which one of the many wise and beautiful verses in the Bible is the greatest. The Jewish scholar Rabbi Akiva argued that the greatest single verse appears in the book of Leviticus:

Thou shalt love thy neighbor as thyself.

The rabbi explained, "Without love of our fellowman, the world would become one vast jungle. The hand of each man would be raised against that of his fellowman."

Jesus, too, selected this verse as the ideal credo of man:

Thou shalt love thy God, and thou shalt love thy neighbor as thyself.

DISCREDIT

Refuse to believe; damage to one's reputation, disgrace.

I would discredit the figure he gave as highly exaggerated; his tendency to exaggeration discredits almost everything he says.

CREDITOR

Someone to whom a debt is owned; someone who believed in you enough to lend you money.

After he won the lottery, all his creditors came to see him collect his winnings.

CREDULOUS

Too ready to believe, easily convinced.

The patent medicine hawker held the credulous crowd spellbound.

CREDENTIAL

A letter of introduction; references.

He appeared for the interview with all his credentials in hand.

CREDENCE

Belief in the report of another.

Fortunately for Mary, her mother didn't put any credence in the rumors she heard about Mary's behavior in school.

CREDITABLE

Praiseworthy, deserving approval.

Despite the fact that she was given very little advance notice, the stand-in actress did a very creditable job in the role.

CREDIBLE

Worthy of belief, trustworthy, reliable.

Mary's explanation of her behavior in school was completely credible to her mother.

CREDO

A belief.

It is very difficult to live by the Christian credo of "Turn the other cheek."

WORDS COME IN FAMILIES   69

CREDIT

Belief in a person; praise or approval for merit; good reputation; in business—sum placed at someone's disposal; in accounting—acknowledgement of payment.

It is to his credit that he did not exhaust all the credit that the bank extended to him.

In education—a unit of study.

John only needs a few more credits to earn his high school diploma.

CREED

A belief; a statement of religious belief; a set of opinions on a subject.

A socialist creed is that all should have an equal share of wealth.

INCREDIBLE

Unbelievable, surprising.

Just a short while ago, it seemed incredible that a man could travel to the moon.

CUR   COURSE

Meaning: To run.

Origin: Latin, *cursus*, *currere*, to run.

We live in a dynamic society. Nothing remains static, especially not ideas. A thought *races* through our minds, fear *stalks* the land; a wave of depression *sweeps* across the country. It is interesting to see how the purely physical act of running (from the root ''cur'') is applied in so many non-physical ways.

For example, when you CONCUR, or *agree,* you are literally *running together with.*

When you pursue a certain COURSE of study at a university, the course is really *the road or way on which you have chosen to run.*

When something OCCURS to you, or *befalls* you, it really means *something has run before you or across your path.*

CURRENT

Running or in progress now; generally accepted, prevalent.

Current beliefs and behavior in regard to sex are in sharp contrast with those of the past.

A flow of water, air, or electricity.

It was difficult to row against the current.

He shut off the electric current before he changed the bulb.

CONCUR

To run together; to happen at the same time; to agree.

They concurred to change the date of the party because it concurred with the date that we were due to sail for Europe.

COURSE

The road or way on which one runs, the direction taken; a series or development; a division of a meal; to run.

In the course of playing on the golf course he felt the blood coursing through his heart and he regretted having had a four-course lunch.

CURSIVE

Running; writing in which the letters are joined.

The teacher wrote on the blackboard in a most beautiful cursive handwriting.

PRECURSOR

A forerunner, a predecessor.

The megaphone was the precursor of the microphone.

RECOURSE

Running or turning to for aid, resorting to.

He tried at first to get back the money owed him without recourse to the law.

RECUR

To happen again, to be repeated.

He was worried that his illness had not been cured and would recur.

INCUR

To run or fall into; to bring upon oneself.

He incurred his father's wrath by borrowing the family car and smashing it up.

CURSORY

Hastily run over, superficial, without attention to details.

A cursory glance at the homework paper showed the teacher that the pupil had made only a cursory effort to do the assignment.

COURIER

Someone who runs errands, a messenger.

The motto of the Main Post Office in New York City is: "Neither snow, nor rain, nor heat, nor gloom of night stays these couriers from the swift completion of their appointed rounds."

CURRICULUM

A course of study.

The curriculum in some progressive schools places as much emphasis on creativity as on content.

CURRENCY

Money passing from hand to hand.

They had to convert their currency each time they came to a new country.

AU COURANT

Running with the current, fully informed, up-to-date.

The theater critic prided himself on being au courant with all the innovations of experimental theater.

DISCURSIVE

Running on from one topic to another, rambling.

He did not seem to be well enough prepared, and his discursive lecture was more confusing than enlightening.

CONCOURSE

A running or gathering together; a broad thoroughfare or boulevard.

The old people liked to gather together on the benches that lined the concourse.

INCURSION

A hostile running in, an intrusion, invasion.

He regarded his mother-in-law's unsolicited advice as an incursion into his marriage.

EXCURSION

A short journey, a pleasure trip.

With packs on their backs, the Boy Scouts were ready for their excursion into the woods.

DISCOURSE

A running conversation, a speech, lecture, dissertation.

The linguistics professor gave a lengthy discourse on the origin and history of the alphabet.

OCCUR

To befall, to take place, happen; to come to mind.

It occurred to him that the accident had occurred because of some defect in the car.

C U R A

Meaning: To cure; to care for.

Origin: Latin, *cura*, care, concern.

INCURABLE is a dreadful word. It proffers no hope; it means very simply: *cannot be cured.*

Through medical research, cures have been found for many diseases which were once thought to be incurable. Tuberculosis, or "consumption," as it was known, claimed the lives of millions of people long ago. In modern times, drugs have been discovered which effectively treat this once dread disease. Indeed, in the first half of this century, deaths from tuberculosis were reduced 95 percent in the United States.

INSURE

To make safe; to guard against harm or loss.

Carrying an umbrella at all times insures you against unpredicted rain.

SINECURE

A job that involves no work or responsibility or care.

His job in his father's business was nothing but a sinecure.

CURIOUS

Caring to learn, eager to know.

A curious child may get into trouble, but he will learn a lot.

CURATOR

A person who cares for, is in charge of, a museum or library.

The curator told the museum guard that the painting was a fake.

ACCURATE

Careful, precise, free of error.

In working with figures, one should be accurate.

CURATE

One responsible for the care of souls; a clergyman who assists a vicar or rector.

The curate prepared the church for the Easter service.

INCURABLE

Cannot be cured or remedied.

Some people believe in euthanasia, or painless killing, for those who are suffering from incurable diseases.

ASSURE

Make someone feel safe; give confidence to; convince.

The parents assured their fearful son that they would not leave the house.

MANICURE

Care of the hands; cleaning, trimming, polishing the fingernails.

While she was waiting for her hair to dry, she decided she might as well have a manicure.

PEDICURE

Care of the foot; cleaning, cutting, polishing the toenails.

Before she would wear open-toed sandals, she went to the beauty parlor for a pedicure.

SECURE

Free from care, safe from harm; strong; firm; to acquire.

He secured a burglar alarm in order to secure himself against robbery.

PROCURE

To obtain by care or effort, to acquire .

He searched around for a long time to procure the exact desk he wanted.

ASSURANCE

Freedom from concern or anxiety, self-confidence; a guarantee; something that dispels doubt or care.

His assurance improved visibly when he was given every assurance that he would be given ample warning.

CURE

Restore to health, heal, remedy.

Throughout the ages man has sought a cure for old age, but so far the only cure is early death.

INSURANCE

Protection against loss by fire, accident, illness, death.

No-fault insurance guarantees compensation regardless of who caused the accident.

CYCLO

Meaning: A circle.

Origin: Latin, *cyclus*, circle.
Greek, *kyklos*, circle, ring.

A wheel is a CIRCULAR frame revolving on an axis. Today, we take wheels for granted, but there was a time when the wheel did not exist. Wearily, men carried their burdens on their backs or dragged them along on the ground.

And then, one of the greatest inventions of all time was made by an unknown genius. Perhaps a fallen tree or a heavy rock started rolling down a mountainside, giving someone the notion of creating the wheel.

The most ancient wheels were pieces cut from smooth round trees. These primitive wheels freed man from being a beast of burden.

CIRCULAR

Round, in the shape of a circle.

One of the things that made the house attractive was that it had a circular staircase.

BICYCLE

A vehicle with two wheels propelled by foot pedals.

During the War, many people rode bicycles instead of cars to preserve gas.

CIRCUS

A circular area for acrobatic, clown, and trained animal performances.

All the children loved the trained seals at the circus.

CIRCUS

A circular area.

Picadilly Circus (or circle) is the Times Square of London.

MOTORCYCLE

A two-wheeled vehicle propelled by an engine.

He always wore a helmet when he rode his motorcycle.

TRICYCLE

A three-wheeled vehicle operated by foot pedals.

Many young children and older people like to ride tricycles.

CIRCLE

A ring; a figure bounded by a single curved line every point of which is equally distant from the center.

The children formed a circle to play the game.

A group of people with common interests.

John is uncomfortable with strangers, but at ease in the circle of his friends.

CYCLIC

Moving in recurrent circles.

In our economy, prosperity and depression follow each other in cyclic fashion.

ENCYCLOPEDIA

A book or set of books with information in all branches of knowledge.

With access to a good encyclopedia, an ambitious person could become self-educated.

ENCYCLICAL

A letter sent by the Pope to large numbers of the clergy.

The Pope recently issued an important encyclical in which he said that the Jews had no share in the guilt for the crucifixion of Jesus.

CYCLONE

A storm in which the wind whirls around and around in a circle.

Cyclones do a great deal of damage in Southern and Central America.

CIRCULATE

To move around in a circle.

The blood circulates throughout the body by way of arteries and veins.

To be distributed to a circle of readers.

A popular book may circulate to hundreds of readers.

CYCLE

A recurrent period of years; a recurrent succession of events.

Joseph interpreted Pharaoh's dream of the seven lean cows devouring the seven fat cows to mean that there would be a seven-year cycle of plenty followed by a seven-year cycle of famine.

D E R M A

Meaning: Skin.

Origin: Greek, *derma*, skin.

The DERMATOLOGIST is *a medical specialist who treats trouble relating to the skin.* This is no easy task, as there are some four hundred separate diseases that can affect the skin.

For young people, the commonest of all the skin troubles is acne. Usually, sprouting pimples is just a sign of adolescence, but sometimes the condition persists. Dermatologists have made great advances in treating acne with antibiotics.

TAXIDERMY

Arranging and mounting the skins of animals.

After studying taxidermy for several years, the hunter was able to mount his hunting trophies and then display them on the wall.

HYPODERMIC

Under the skin.

Sometimes a doctor will give a patient a hypodermic injection to ward off disease.

DERMATOLOGIST

Skin specialist.

Some dermatologists recommend salt-water bathing for people suffering from the skin disease called psoriasis.

EPIDERMIS

The outer layer of the skin.

A daily bath or shower is important in order to keep the epidermis clean.

PACHYDERM

An animal with a very thick skin such as an elephant, hippopotamus, or rhinoceros.

A light bullet would bounce off the skin of a pachyderm.

D I C

Meaning: To say, to speak.

Origin: Latin, *dicere*, to speak, to say.

There was a time when people existed without speaking. They cried in terror, or pain; they smiled and frowned; they screamed and gestured. *But they had no words.*

And then—exactly how it happened we will never know—language was born. The first word uttered by man was a momentous act of invention.

Possibly, the first words uttered were the names of animals, and were simply imitations of the sounds the animals made. A lion might have been called something like *rara,* a snake, *sssss,* a bird, *tsip, tsip.* Then, perhaps some early men realized it would be useful for them to agree on what to call all the things that they could see. As language developed in time, this simple naming of things was joined by the more complicated naming of intangibles—of ideas and feelings.

Of all the many thousands of species of living things, man alone has developed this great gift of speech. Man has tried to teach language to other species with some limited measure of success.

The celebrated linguist, Noam Chomsky, tells us that it is in the physiological and neurological nature of man to develop spoken language. Every human being has this potential which, unless impeded in some way, develops in the normal course of human growth. Even people born deaf, who do not automatically develop speech because they do not hear it, can develop language and can be taught to speak.

VERDICT

Formal response or finding of a jury; judgment, decision.

When the jury's verdict of "not guilty" was announced, the defendant fainted with relief.

BENEDICTION

A blessing; literally, a speaking well of.

The priest gave a benediction at the beginning of the banquet.

DICTION

Manner of speaking.

The actor's rich voice and excellent diction made every word of the play clearly understandable.

DICTATE

To speak for someone else to write down; to command or impose orders on.

The secretary typed up the letters which her boss had dictated to her.

PREDICT

To tell in advance what will happen.

All through the ages, astrologers have tried to predict what will happen from the pattern of the stars.

ABDICATE

To renounce, to give up a throne or high office, to say it is no longer yours.

King Edward VIII of England abdicated his throne in order to marry Wallis Simpson.

CONTRADICT

To declare that something is incorrect or untrue; literally, to speak against.

Johnny's mother was furious with him for contradicting her when she stated her age.

DICTATOR

A ruler with absolute power; a person whose word must be obeyed.

After suffering many years of cruelty and injustice, the people revolted against their dictator.

EDICT

An order proclaimed by authority, a decree: literally, a speaking out.

The revocation in 1685 of Henry IV's Edict of Nantes, which had granted political equality to the Huguenots, led to the persecution of the Protestants.

DICTIONARY

A book of alphabetically listed words and their meanings.

The third edition of the great Webster dictionary created quite a sensation because it listed many usages and meanings formerly considered improper. The editor defended himself, explaining that the dictionary is not there to dictate, but is merely a record of what people say.

DICTUM

A saying, an utterance.

Popular along Broadway was the dictum "Gentlemen prefer blondes."

D U C

Meaning: To lead.

Origin: Latin, *ducere*, to lead.

Man's continued existence on this earth is made possible by his ability to PRODUCE, that is, *to bring forth enough to feed and clothe himself.*

There was a time when man depended on hunting for food. He was forced to live a nomadic life, following game wherever it went. And if the prey eluded the hunter, man went hungry.

Then the miraculous discovery was made that if seeds were sown, grain would grow. Grain could be pounded and roasted and thus made into bread to nourish man. Hunting animals in the forest no longer had such desperate urgency. Instead of traveling from place to place, men settled down to tend their crops.

For many thousands of years, man had to cut down the ripened grain by hand. A strong man could harvest but two acres in a day of hard labor.

In 1846, Cyrus McCormick invented the reaper, which harvested grain by machine. With this machine, one man could do the work formerly done by twenty. McCormick's original reaper is now in a museum, where it looks to us like a big clumsy toy. But the reaper was a major advance in man's ability to produce his own food.

CONDUCIVE

Leading to, contributing to.

A quiet, orderly room is conducive to studying.

IL DUCE

The leader (Italian).

Mussolini, the Fascist leader of Italy, was known as Il Duce.

DEDUCE

To draw a conclusion, to infer.

The word deduce *was made famous by Sherlock Holmes, who was always making deductions from the clues that his sharp eye observed.*

AQUEDUCT

A large pipe or channel for bringing water from a distance.

New York City gets most of its fresh water from the Catskill and the Croton Aqueducts.

REPRODUCE

To bring forth again or anew.

Man's uncontrolled ability to reproduce has created the threat of overpopulation.

REPRODUCTION

A copy; the process of creating new life.

The art dealer said that the painting was a reproduction, not an original.

VIADUCT

A bridge for carrying a road or railroad over a valley or gorge.

A viaduct was built to enable the road to continue over the swampy land.

DUCT

A tube, pipe, channel.

The glands in the body which have ducts empty into organs, whereas the ductless glands send their secretions directly into the blood.

PRODUCE

To bring forth, to create; to cause.

His suggestion for changing the curriculum produced both positive and negative responses from the students.

To present on the screen or stage.

Having been an actor for many years, he now wanted to produce and direct his own play.

CONDUCT

To lead, to direct.

The chairman tried to conduct the meeting in a democratic fashion, giving everyone a chance to participate.

Behavior, deportment.

He was an excellent student, and received good marks on his report card for both his studies and his conduct.

INDUCTIVE

Reasoning from the specific to the general.

Young children usually learn language by inductive reasoning, proceeding from many examples of usage to the general grammatical rule.

REDUCE

To lead back, to lower, lessen, diminish.

The scientists have said that the lean rats bury the fat rats, which is their way of saying that if you are overweight you had better reduce if you want to live long.

EDUCATE

To lead out, to bring out someone's powers, capacities, and talents.

To educate is not just to pour in material for students to learn; by definition, education means developing the latent powers of students.

DEDUCTIVE

Reasoning from the general to the specific.

Knowing that hot air rises, he concluded by deductive reasoning that sitting upstairs would be uncomfortably hot.

SEDUCE

To lead away from the right path.

She thought that being flirtatious would be seductive, but instead of being seduced he was repelled.

PRODUCT

Something created by nature or by man.

The furniture factory turns out thousands of products every week.

Result.

An unhappy child is often the product of an unhappy marriage.

Number obtained by multiplication.

Forty is the product of eight and five.

DUKE

A high-ranking nobleman who is quite close to the royal family.

When Edward VIII abdicated the throne, he retained his title as Duke of Windsor.

INTRODUCE

To lead or bring in.

The visiting professor introduced many new ideas into the university.

To present to.

The child introduced his mother to the teacher.

INDUCE

To lead into beliefs or actions; to persuade.

Despite all my pleading and arguing, I could not induce him to change his mind.

To cause or bring about.

Sometimes, doctors induce labor during a pregnancy because they judge the baby is overdue.

EMPT EMERE

Meaning: To buy, to take.

Origin: Latin, *empt*, *emere*, to buy, to take.

There is a famous Latin proverb, "caveat emptor," which means *Let the buyer beware*. The phrase cautions the buyer to be very careful when he purchases goods.

Recently, much progress has been made in the area of consumer protection. Most stores will readily accept returns of goods the customer is not satisfied with. The consumer is also protected by law. He has recourse to government agencies and to better business bureaus if he thinks he has suffered an injustice.

Nevertheless, so common has the saying become that the word CAVEAT has persisted as a noun in English. A CAVEAT means a *warning,* or a *caution*.

EXAMPLE

What you take out to copy or imitate, a model, something that shows what the rest is like.

The famous Nôtre Dame Cathedral in Paris is an example of Gothic architecture.

PEREMPTORY

Arbitrary, dogmatic, taking a position that leaves no choice.

He announced his decision in a peremptory manner and would allow no discussion.

PREEMPT

To acquire or to seize something beforehand.

When the West was being settled, cattle owners would preempt thousands of acres of land for their herds to graze.

PROMPT

Ready, quick.

He received a prompt reply to his letter.

On time.

Mary is always prompt in doing her homework.

To inspire.

The teacher's encouraging words prompted the student to work even harder.

To remind.

At the early rehearsals, the actors needed prompting to remember lines.

REDEEM

To buy back; to set free by paying ransom; to convert into cash.

He needed cash, so he redeemed some of the stocks and bonds he owned.

To compensate for.

After behaving rudely on their first date, he redeemed himself by sending flowers and candy before their next date.

EXEMPT

To take out, to remove, to free from the rule.

He was exempted from the final examination because of the excellent work he had done all term long.

SAMPLE

A part that illustrates the whole, an example.

She took a small sample of the material she had selected for the sofa to show to her husband.

RANSOM

Money paid to free a captive.

The distraught parents agreed to pay the ransom required by the kidnappers for the return of their child.

PREMIUM

A bonus, a gift, a sum additional to the price or wages that are paid.

Many companies give out premiums to encourage consumers to buy their products.

E Q U I

Meaning: Equal.

Origin: Latin, *equi*, equal.

Did you ever stop to wonder why the great circle around the center of the earth is called the EQUATOR? The equator is so called because it divides the world into two equal halves; hence its derivation from the root which means *equal*.

The equator, of course, is an imaginary line. Drawn halfway between the North Pole and the South Pole, it divides the surface of the earth into the Northern Hemisphere and the Southern Hemisphere.

The South American country, Ecuador, is so called because it straddles the equator.

EQUILIBRIUM

A well-balanced condition, in which each side has equal weight.

He is a very stable person and does not lose his equilibrium even when he is deliberately provoked.

EQUANIMITY

Evenness of temper, of spirit.

The customer maintained his equanimity even when the waiter poured soup all over him.

EQUINOX

Time when the sun crosses the equator.

On the two equinox days in our calendar, March 21 and September 22, day and night are exactly equal all over the earth.

EQUALITY

Being equal.

The Women's Lib(eration) movement seeks to achieve equality for women politically, economically, and socially.

EQUIVALENT

Equal, having the same value.

To a starving man, a loaf of bread is equivalent to a magnificent feast.

INIQUITY

Lack of equality or justice; wickedness, sinfulness.

The civil rights movement seeks to correct the terrible iniquities suffered by Blacks in America.

EQUIVOCAL

Uncertain, having more than one meaning.

Someone who is equivocal talks out of both sides of his mouth and is deliberately misleading.

EQUATE

To treat as equal.

When the United Nations equated Zionism with racism, many people regarded the move as a deliberate distortion for political ends.

EQUATION

An expression of equality between two quantities.

We learned to solve simple equations, such as $X + 3 = 8$, in beginning algebra.

EQUITABLE

Fair, just.

When the old man died, his will made an equitable distribution of his possessions among the members of his family.

ADEQUATE

Equal to the task, sufficient.

As a student, John exerts a minimum of effort and does an adequate, but in no way exceptional, job.

FACT FECT

Meaning: To do.

Origin: Latin, *facere*, to do.

The derivation of the word MANUFACTURED seems to contain a contradiction. If we take the word apart—"manu" means *hand*, and "fact" means *to do*—it would seem to mean *handmade*. However, the word MANUFACTURE brings to mind the production of goods on a large scale, using complicated machinery. To unravel this contradiction, we have to go back in history.

There was a time when the FACTORY, *the place where things were made,* was located in the home. There, all things were really made by hand by the family. In time, the factory was moved out of the home. People, who were not related, were given raw materials and worked side by side to create finished products—by hand. Gradually, people began to invent machines to do the work that was being painstakingly done by hand.

Today, of course, things are made by machinery on a gigantic scale. If something is actually made by hand, it is clearly labeled "handmade," to distinguish it from manufactured or machine-made products.

DEFECT

A shortcoming, a deficiency.

Many articles are guaranteed against defects and can be returned within a given period of time.

AFFECT

To influence; to make someone feel something.

Shortening the school day may affect the students' achievement and delay their graduation.

DEFICIENT

Wanting in something, incomplete, defective.

Sailors on long voyages often contracted scurvy, a disease resulting from a deficient intake of vitamin C.

DEFEAT

To ruin, destroy, frustrate, beat.

The school's basketball team is not very good and is defeated in every contest.

DIFFICULT

Not easy, hard.

John is very good in math, but he finds history his most difficult subject.

EFFECT

Influence; result.

His determination to work harder had a positive effect on his grades.

EFFICIENT

Working well, capable.

Mary is an efficient typist and does her work neatly and accurately.

FACILITY

Ease; skill.

He was very outgoing and had a great facility for making friends.

Means for doing something.

The building was not complete and had no bathroom facilities as yet.

FACULTY

Ability, natural power.

Mary is very diplomatic and has an unusual faculty for saying the right thing at the right time.

All the teachers on a staff.

There was a faculty meeting to discuss teachers' salaries.

FEAT

Something done.

The young man who threw a wire across the two buildings of the World Trade Center, 1300 feet up in the air, and very calmly walked across it, accomplished an amazing, but illegal, feat.

FACTORY

A place where things are made or manufactured.

John's father works on the assembly line in an automobile factory.

FEATURE

A distinct part.

One of her best features is her long golden hair.

A special story in a newspaper or magazine.

The feature story dealt with the kidnapping of the heiress.

A full-length movie; to make outstanding.

There was a double feature at the movie house, featuring the same actress in both films.

FACSIMILE

An exact copy.

He was asked to send a facsimile of his birth certificate along with his application.

FACTION

A small group of dissenters within an organization.

The Student Council split into factions on the issue of grading.

FACTOR

Element, condition.

When it involved his child's health, money was no factor, and he was willing to spend all his savings to get adequate medical care.

FACT

A deed, something that has happened, or is true.

Although in everybody's opinion John is the best swimmer in the school, the fact is that he only came in second in the swimming match.

FACILITATE

To make easier, to help.

Busing children to schools outside their neighborhoods may facilitate desegregation, but it leaves other problems unsolved.

FAM   FANT   FAB

Meaning: To speak.

Origin: Latin, *fari*, to speak.

At birth, the senses of an INFANT operate on a fundamental level. He can see, hear, taste, feel, and smell to some degree. As the child grows older, these senses develop more fully.

What an infant *cannot* do at birth, however, is speak. Though each person is born with the ability to speak, he must learn how.

INFANTICIDE, the killing of babies, was practiced widely by the Greeks and other ancient peoples, with the notable exception of the ancient Hebrews.

In ancient times as well as today, murder of any kind was, of course, anathema to the Judeo-Christian ethic. The killing of infants—helpless human beings—was especially shocking.

Today, orthodox Catholics and Jews regard abortion as infanticide, and they strictly oppose it.

FABLE

A story about animals told to teach a moral lesson; a myth, legend.

Aesop's fables have given us such useful expressions and sayings as "sour grapes," and "one good turn deserves another."

INEFFABLE

Inexpressible; so exalted that it cannot be uttered; words cannot tell or describe it.

He was overwhelmed with emotion at the death of his mother and poured his ineffable feelings into his painting.

FAMOUS

Being well known or much talked about, renowned.

Many tourists flock to see the famous Eiffel Tower in Paris.

INFANT

One who cannot speak, a very young child, a baby.

The five-year-old was very spoiled and cried like an infant whenever she couldn't have her way.

INFAMOUS

Having a bad reputation, wicked, in dishonor.

Benedict Arnold, an American Revolutionary general, was guilty of the infamous crime of treason.

INFANTRY

Foot soldiers.

Traditionally, the young men who were not experienced enough to ride horses in the cavalry joined the infantry.

FABULOUS

Legendary, incredible, astounding.

His business grew increasingly profitable, earning him fabulous wealth.

PREFACE

An introduction to a book.

In the preface, the author generally tells why he wrote the book.

FATE

What is destined to happen.

The Romans had an ancient belief that fate was the sentence of the gods; whatever the gods spoke was what would happen to you.

F E R

Meaning: To carry.

Origin: Latin, *ferre*, to carry, to bear.

When we describe something as FERTILE, we mean it *brings forth in abundance*. Fertile land bears rich crops in great quantities. A fertile woman is capable of producing many children. A fertile mind produces many ideas.

Fertility was extremely important to primitive man. To assure his day-to-day existence, he required a constant supply of food. Equally vital was the continuous birth of children to ensure the survival of the race.

Fertility rites to encourage productivity of the land and of its people were a part of every primitive culture. Dances, prayers, ritual sacrifices, dolls, and idols were created to mollify the gods and affect the unpredictable forces of nature. Some of these ancient practices continue in modified form in our modern civilization. The Maypole dance is one such spring ritual.

OFFER

To present for acceptance or refusal; proposal.

George Washington Carver, the great American Negro agricultural scientist, offered his life savings to the Tuskegee Institute, where he was the director of agricultural research.

PREFER

To put something before something else; to regard a thing as being more important than something else.

The early Christians in Rome preferred to die rather than give up their faith.

DIFFER

To disagree.

The newlyweds differed about what style of furniture they wanted.

DIFFER

To be unlike.

Their outfits differed only in the neckline.

REFER

To carry back something, to turn attention to; to apply.

In order to type a complicated chart, a clerk may refer to his typing manual.

INFER

To draw as a conclusion, imply.

If a woman puts Ms. in front of her name, it can be inferred that her marital status is no one's business.

DEFERENCE

Submitting or yielding courteous respect.

He didn't agree, but he deferred to the opinion of his grandfather in deference to his age.

TRANSFER

To carry or change from one place to another.

When they moved, the children had to transfer to the school in their new neighborhood.

CONFER

To bring together for discussion.

The students asked to confer with the teachers about the gym program.

SUFFER

To be afflicted with, endure.

Some people are in favor of mercy killing for those who suffer from incurable diseases.

Bear, allow.

Since Mary would not suffer her supervisor's humiliating treatment, she began to look for a new job.

REFERENDUM

Carrying a proposal directly to the people.

There was a movement to remove the president from his office by referendum.

FERTILIZE

To make productive.

Many chemicals used to fertilize the soil are now regarded as dangerous pollutants.

F I D

Meaning: Having faith.

Origin: Latin, *fides*, trust.

FIDELITY, or *faithfulness* is commonly regarded as one of the great virtues of life. To have faith, whether in God or in one's fellow-man, is an important guiding principle.

Faith can be used to mean an *organized religion,* as the Catholic *faith,* or the Moslem *faith.* When we say that someone has faith, we mean he has an unquestioning belief in his God and in his religion.

We can also use the word FAITH to describe someone's feelings about another person or thing. Then we are talking about *trust, confidence,* and *loyalty.*

Some of the most beautiful stories in literature depict man's fidelity. In the *Aeneid,* the famous Latin epic poem by Virgil, there is a touching story of Achates, the loyal friend of Aeneas. The beautiful and well-known Biblical story of Ruth tells of a Moabite woman's faithfulness to her mother-in-law, Naomi.

FIDUCIARY

Relating to someone who holds something in trust for someone.

When the parents were killed in an automobile accident, the uncle held their estate in fiduciary trust for their young son.

DIFFIDENT

Lacking faith or confidence in oneself, shy.

He was diffident about accepting the nomination because he felt that he did not have sufficient experience for the office.

CONFIDE

To have trust in, to share private matters or secrets.

Mary was very relieved when she was able to confide her troubles to her mother.

BONAFIDE

In good faith, honest, authentic.

He was assured that the dog he wanted to buy was pedigreed, with bonafide papers to prove it.

CONFIDENCE

Trust, assurance; belief in one's own abilities.

Because her parents had confidence in her, Mary became self-confidant.

DEFY

To renounce allegiance to, to challenge the power of, to resist.

Joan of Arc defied the English invaders of France, but her defiance led to her doom.

SEMPER FIDELIS

Always faithful.

The motto of the United States Marine Corps is SEMPER FIDELIS.

PERFIDY

A breach of faith, treachery.

After their divorce, she was shocked at his perfidy in revealing the most personal things about her to their friends.

INFIDEL

One without faith, a person who does not believe in a certain religion; heathen, pagan.

Many missionaries went to Africa to convert the native infidels to Christianity.

FIDELITY

Faithfulness, devotion to one's vows.

Fidelity in marriage is a commandment that is frequently violated.

Accurate reproduction.

He bought a stereo phonograph to achieve greater sound fidelity.

FLECT FLEX

Meaning: To bend.

Origin: Latin, *flexus*, to bend.

The sun and the moon offer a dramatic example of the word REFLECTION. The light we see shining from the moon is actually the reflection of light from the sun. Light waves hit the surface of the moon and are reflected, or "bent back" to be observed by us on earth.

Ancient people made use of the sun and the moon in recording the passage of time. Obviously, the rising and setting of the sun indicated the passing of each day. The ancients also observed the regular way in which the moon grew from a thin, silvery crescent to a full, round, and fairly golden ball, and then once again gradually faded away to a sliver.

In ancient Babylon, it was noted that this cycle took 29½ days. The cycle occurred with such utter regularity, that the Babylonians called this block of time a "moon." In English, of course, the word MONTH comes from the word "moon."

FLEXIBLE

Easily bent, pliant.

Tamar's parents hoped that she would become a dancer because she had such a flexible body.

FLEXIBLE

Easily adaptable to change.

His schedule is very flexible and he can go out to lunch whenever it is convenient for him.

DEFLECT

To bend or turn aside, swerve.

The policeman wore a bulletproof vest which deflected the bullets of the terrorists.

FLEX

To bend, to contract a muscle.

The strong man in the circus flexed his powerful muscles, making them bend and ripple.

REFLECT

To throw back light; to give back an image.

His nervousness was reflected in the way he kept clasping and unclasping his hands.

To think seriously.

He didn't accept the job offer right away because he wanted time to reflect on it.

REFLEX

A bending back, as an involuntary or instinctive reaction.

Blinking is a reflex action to protect the eye against dust or dirt.

FUND FUS

Meaning: To pour or melt metal or glass.

Origin: Latin, *fundere*, to pour.

A FOUNDRY is a place where metals are melted down. This is the story, as far as we can reconstruct it, of how the world's first foundry came to be:

During the Stone Age, all weapons and tools were made of stone. In the Old Stone Age, the weapons were quite crude; in the New Stone Age, weapons were sharper, more polished, and more efficient. To this day, some primitive tribes still live in the Stone Age.

Imagine a group of men sitting around a fire about 6,000 years ago. They notice something red and shiny pouring out of the hot green stones from their fireplace. It is copper, melted out of the copper ore in the stones. The primitive men are fascinated by the substance and try to find a use for it.

At first, they merely use the cooled pieces of ore as ornaments. But they quickly realize the usefulness of the copper, and they start making tools and weapons from it. They make hotter fires to get more and more of the shining stuff out of the stone.

Copper is fairly soft. When tin is added to copper, the result is bronze, a much harder substance. After early man realized this, he began melting and fusing the two materials together.

The age of metals had begun.

FUSION

A pouring together, a union as if by melting.

A good theatrical production requires a fusion of many talents.

PROFUSE

Abundant, as though pouring forth.

He was profuse in his apologies for having come late.

FUNNEL

A cone-shaped tube for pouring liquids into a small opening.

We used a funnel to pour the wine back into the bottle.

REFUND

To give money back.

The department store announced a final sale in which prices would be very low, but the store would not refund any customer's money.

CONFUSE

To mix up, bewilder.

The teacher tried to explain Einstein's Theory of Relativity, but the class remained completely confused.

Mistake the identity of.

The man greeted me as though he knew me, but actually he had confused me with someone else.

INFUSE

To inspire.

After seeing the beautiful ballet performance, she was infused with such enthusiasm she decided to take dancing lessons.

To pour in.

After the operation, the patient was fed intravenously; glucose was infused directly into his bloodstream.

WORDS COME IN FAMILIES 113

TRANSFUSION

Pouring blood across from one person to another.

He lost a great deal of blood in the operation and needed several transfusions.

CONFOUNDED

So poured together that the separate elements cannot be identified, all mixed up, thrown into confusion.

His strange and erratic behavior amazed and confounded us.

This word is sometimes used as a mild swear word, as in:

He is a confounded nuisance.

DIFFUSE

Poured in different directions, not concentrated; wordy.

His explanation was diffuse and we remained as puzzled as before.

SUFFUSE

Spread over with liquid, light, color.

The setting sun suffused the sky with the most beautiful colors.

FUSE

To melt; to unite by melting; a device for setting off explosives; a wire used as a safeguard in an electrical circuit.

When the electrical wiring is overloaded, the fuse blows, breaking the circuit and preventing fire.

FUND

Meaning: Source, basis.

Origin: Latin, *fundus*, bottom.

The Latin word "fundere," meaning *to pour metal,* is not to be confused with a similar Latin word, "fundare," meaning *to base.* In the first case, there is a process of fusion of different elements; whereas in the second case, a bottom is being laid for something to be built upon.

It does make you wonder, however, whether the term FOUNDING FATHERS refers to the men who not only laid the basis for our nation, but who also fused diverse peoples into a united state.

FOUNDER

A person who establishes.

Alexander Graham Bell, the inventor of the telephone, was the founder of the Bell Telephone Company.

To fall to the bottom, to fail, to break down.

John had been doing very well in school, but after his prolonged absence due to illness, his work began to founder.

FOUND

To lay the basis; to establish.

Harvard University, the oldest American college, was founded in 1636.

FOUNDATION

The supporting part of a building.

Before they started building their new house, they made sure the foundation was solid.

The principle or idea upon which something is based.

The foundation of a democracy is the belief that everyone has equal rights.

A fund to maintain an institution or charity.

The Ford Foundation supports many cultural and charitable institutions with generous gifts of money.

PROFOUND

Very deep.

He knew a great deal about film-making and his analysis of the new movie was profound.

Intense.

Going to college away from home made a profound change in her personality.

FUNDAMENTAL

Basic, essential.

Knowing how to swim is fundamental for a sailor.

An underlying principle.

The fundamental reason for his not being accepted into college was that he did not know the fundamentals of math.

FUND

A supply.

He is a sports enthusiast and has a fund of information about every athlete and every sports contest.

A sum of money.

The school library has very limited funds for the purchase of new books.

GENUS

Meaning: Race, kind, species, birth.

Origin: Latin, *genus*, *generis*, race, kind, class.
Latin, *generare*, to beget, produce.

GENESIS, the first book of the Old Testament, gives an account of the creation of the universe and the origin of man. The following verse comes from Genesis:

This is the book of the generations of Adam.

Some rabbis have considered this as the most important verse in the Bible, because the declaration indicates that all men come from one source and are part of one large indistinguishable human family. It follows, then, that each person ought to treat every other person as his brother.

The word root "genus" speaks of birth, of the begetting of generation after generation. Ironically, there is another word, which, though it has the same root, "gen," deals with a death-producing, not a life-producing substance. This fearful word is CARCINOGEN.

causes and cure of cancer, are now more and more convinced that this dread disease is brought about by substances in our environment. They call these substances carcinogens.

For example, it has been proven that cigarettes contain many carcinogens. Yet every year, tens of thousands of students join the ranks of cigarette smokers. Can it be they value themselves so little they rush headlong to their own destruction?

GENRE

Type, kind, style.

The movie "2001" is in the genre of science fiction.

PROGENITOR

A forefather, ancestor.

Adam was the progenitor of the whole human race.

GENERATION

All the people born or living in the same period of time.

Sometimes it is difficult for parents and children to communicate with each other because of the generation gap.

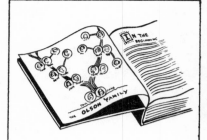

GENEALOGY

The story of descent from a common ancestor, the study of family lineage.

It is a common practice for families to draw their genealogy, or family tree, in the first page of their Bible.

DEGENERATE

To change to a lower type; deteriorate.

Cruel and inhumane conditions in many prisons cause the inmates to degenerate mentally and physically.

CONGENIAL

Sharing the same tastes, agreeable, friendly.

She was happy she had come to the party because she found the people congenial.

GENERAL

Applying to all, common, widespread.

The principal made a general announcement that all students were to leave the school building.

High-ranking army officer.

Before he became President, General Eisenhower served as commander of the Allied Forces in Europe during World War II.

EUGENICS

The science of improving the breed through control of hereditary factors.

Eugenics warns against intermarriage between closely related families when there are physical or mental weaknesses in the family tree.

GENE

Substance in the chromosomes through which inherited characteristics are transmitted from the parents to the offspring.

The sex chromosomes (XX from the mother and XY from the father) carry the genes that determine whether the baby will be male or female.

GENOCIDE

The killing off of a whole people.

The Turks attempted genocide of the Armenians during World War I.

GENIAL

Pleasant, warm friendly, cheerful.

The host had a genial manner and made all his guests feel at home.

GENDER

Classification as masculine, feminine, neuter.

In English grammar, only a few nouns have masculine or feminine gender, but in other languages (such as French, German, Hebrew) all nouns are classified as masculine, feminine, or neuter.

GENITAL

Having to do with reproduction or with the sex organs.

According to Freud, in the third stage of child development (called the "phallic" or "Oedipal stage"), the child becomes more aware of his genital organs.

CONGENITAL

Existing at birth.

The baby was born prematurely and had congenital defects of the hands and feet.

HYDROGEN

A gaseous element used to create water

Water consists of two parts hydrogen and one part oxygen.

PREGNANT

Being "with child" or about to give birth.

The pregnant woman was knitting clothes for the expected baby.

PROGENY

Those to whom we give birth, children, offspring, issue.

The parents gazed with pride at their newly born progeny.

HETEROGENEOUS

Composed of different kinds.

The teacher had to work with the students individually because the class was heterogeneous and had widely varying interests and abilities.

HOMOGENIZE

To make uniform.

When milk is homogenized, the fat particles are finely divided and the cream does not separate from the rest of the milk.

GENIUS

A person with extraordinary natural intellectual or creative powers.

All the world recognizes Albert Einstein as one of the great geniuses of science.

HOMOGENEOUS

Composed of the same kind.

Members of the group got along very well because they were homogeneous in ability and background.

GENEROUS

Acting as well born, willing to give or share, unselfish.

The child was very generous and shared his toys with his friends.

G E O

Meaning: The earth.

Origin: Greek, *geo*, the earth.

In days of old, men believed that the earth was the center of the universe and that the heavenly bodies all revolved around the earth. This belief is described by the word GEOCENTRIC.

In the early sixteenth century, Nicholas Copernicus, a Polish astronomer, proved that the geocentric universe was merely an illusion. He demonstrated beyond all doubt that our earth is just one small planet, and that the earth moves around the sun. He also proved that the earth revolves on its own axis.

Copernicus' revolutionary observations upset his contemporaries. They were more comfortable with Ptolemy's ancient theory that man, created by God, was the center of everything. The intellectual achievement of Copernicus in laying the basis for modern astronomy was utterly fantastic.

Years later, the astronomer Tycho Brahe, looking at the simple wooden instruments with which Copernicus had worked, said these beautiful words in praise of his master:

The earth has not produced such a man for centuries. He has made the immovable earth move around the sun in a circle — he has changed for us the very face of the universe. With these small sticks, he has done what was not permitted to any other mortal to do since the beginning of the world.

GEOMETRY

Measuring the earth, a branch of mathematics dealing with magnitude and space measurements.

Geometry and trigonometry began in ancient Egypt; when the Nile flooded its banks, exact measurements of land were necessary to determine ownership.

GEOLOGY

The science dealing with the earth, its crust, the rocks of which it is composed, and the changes it has undergone.

When Johnny showed interest in his rock collection, his mother assumed he would want to study geology.

GEORGE

A farmer, a man who works the earth.

The two chief contenders in the war of the American Revolution both bore the name George: King George III of England, and George Washington, commander-in-chief of the American army.

GEOPOLITICS

The study of the relation of politics to geography.

Geopolitics indicates that a landlocked nation could not become a world power without a policy of expansionism.

GEOGRAPHY

A description of the surface of the earth.

In his geography class, John learned about the natural resources and chief products of the African countries.

GNOSIS

Meaning: To know.

Origin: Greek, *gnosis*, knowledge.

In the late Hellenistic and early Christian eras, there existed a religious and philosophical movement known as GNOSTICISM. GNOSTICS claimed that they alone had knowledge of certain mystical doctrines which were the only means of man's salvation.

The origins of the Gnostics' beliefs stem from such varied sources as the Greek mystery cults, the Jewish Cabbala, and Egyptian and Babylonian mythology. Some Christian doctrines were also incorporated into Gnosticism, and for this reason, early Christians regarded the Gnostics as dangerous heretics.

COGNOSCENTI

Those who are in the know.

All the cognoscenti flocked to the exhibit of the sculptor's new work.

RECOGNIZE

To know again; to identify.

She had lost so much weight that I hardly recognized her.

To accept.

Sometimes parents find it hard to recognize their children's rights to choose their own careers.

To take notice of; to show appreciation of.

After he had struggled for years to become an actor, his talents were finally recognized.

KNOWLEDGE

Range of information, under-standing, awareness.

He had devoted his life to the study of biology and had a profound knowledge of the workings of the body.

DIAGNOSIS

Identification of disease through the examination of symptoms; careful investigation; decision after examination .

After examining the patient carefully, the doctor's diagnosis was that he had suffered a minor stroke.

CONNOISSEUR

A person who has expert knowledge in some field.

She was afraid to invite her husband's boss to dinner because she had heard he was a connoisseur of fine food.

COGNITION

The process of knowing, awareness.

Cognition is the intellectual process by which knowledge is gained about perceptions or ideas.

PROGNOSIS

Forecast; prediction about the probable course of a disease.

The child was doing very well after his operation and the prognosis was for a full recovery.

AGNOSTIC

A person who says it is impossible to know whether or not God exists.

It has been said that many agnostics find faith when death nears.

G R A D   G R E S

Meaning: To go, to walk, to step.

Origin: Latin, *gradi*, *gress*, to go, to walk.

The root, "grad" or "gres," suggests activity, but the connotation of the root is totally neutral. Various prefixes define the direction of the movement. The result is a family of words with quite varied meanings and connotations, all describing man's directions.

DIGRESS

To deviate from a course or a subject, ramble.

It was very hard to follow the professor's lecture because he frequently disgressed and forgot to come back to his main point.

GRADUATE

One who has finished a course of study; to receive a diploma for completing a course.

Ivan and Natasha had to adjust to school in their new homeland, but they graduated with honors nevertheless.

GRADUAL

Proceeding by degrees.

The immigrant gradually became accustomed to his new homeland.

DEGREE

A step in a process; extent, intensity.

The degree to which he succeeded was directly related to the amount of effort he exerted.

A rank given by a college or university.

He was very proud to receive his LL.D. degree from law school.

Unit of measure for angles and for temperature.

When two straight lines cross perpendicular to each other, a 90 degree or right angle is formed.

INGREDIENT

A component part.

The law requires that all ingredients be listed on every package of food and drugs.

EGRESS

Going out; exit.

The loft had no doors or windows, and the only egress was through a trap door in the floor.

GRADE

Step or degree in rank.

Some people are opposed to giving grades in school because it compares one student with another instead of evaluating each student's own growth.

AGGRESSIVE

Starting fights or quarrels; bold, pushy; exercising initiative.

He did not wait for opportunity to knock at his door but pursued his goals aggressively.

DEGRADE

To lower, to corrupt.

Although he could not get a job in his own profession and had to work as a laborer, he did not feel as degraded as he had felt as a political prisoner.

AGGRESSION

An unprovoked attack.

The United States was accused of acts of aggression in Viet Nam and Cambodia.

TRANSGRESS

To step across a limit or boundary.

People often post signs on their private estates telling outsiders not to transgress on the property.

To go beyond, or break, a law; to depart from the accepted norms of conduct.

Foreign diplomats are allowed to transgress parking regulations.

PROGRESS

Move forward.

The world has made much progress in science and technology, but the problems of poverty and war are still with us.

RETROGRESS

To move backward, to decline.

The child was so nervous about starting to attend kindergarten that he retrogressed and began wetting again at night.

REGRESS

To go or to move backward.

Under stress, people sometimes regress to childlike behavior.

INGRESS

Entrance.

They had to get special permission to gain ingress to the temple.

GRAM GRAPH

Meaning: To write.

Origin: Greek, *gramma*, a letter.
          Greek, *graphein*, to write.

There was a time when sinking ships or ships in trouble had no way of calling for help.

Then, in 1895, Guglielmo Marconi invented the wireless TELEGRAPH. With this startling invention, words could flash their invisible way across thousands of miles of water or land, without benefit of wires. The system Marconi invented made use of the invisible electromagnetic waves that fill the air.

The diligent work of Marconi and other scientists eventually introduced radio and television to all parts of the world. With such revolutionized communication, the world and all its people became more intimately related.

TELEGRAM

A message transmitted by telegraph.

They were happy to receive a telegram saying that their son had arrived safely.

EPIGRAM

A short, witty quotable saying.

An epigram popular in many languages and among many peoples is "Silence is golden."

PROGRAM

A plan of proceedings.

We worked together to arrange a program for the family vacation.

A list of the events of an entertainment.

The parents were thrilled to see their child's name on the program for the class play.

EPIGRAPH

Inscription written on stone, on a building, or on a monument.

Some of the epigraphs that archeologists study are many thousands of years old.

MONOGRAM

A figure made up of the initials of a name combined into a single unit of design.

For her birthday, we gave her monogrammed stationery.

GRAMMAR

The system of word structures and word arrangements of a language; a system of rules for a given language.

When you first learn to speak a new language, you make many mistakes in grammar.

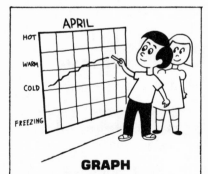

GRAPH

A diagram or chart to show relationship or change.

The children recorded the daily temperature on their graph and could observe the weather trends.

GRAPHIC

Clearly written or told, vivid.

Ilana described her trip in such graphic terms, I felt as though I had been there with her.

PHONOGRAPH

An instrument that reproduces sound from the tracings written on the disc or record.

Although he had difficulty hearing, Grandpa loved to listen to old records on the phonograph.

GREG

Meaning: A flock, herd.

Origin: Latin, *gregis*, *grex*, flock, herd.

The tendency of man to herd together in groups has, unfortunately, led to practices of inclusion and exclusion. Some of the most cruel and unjust conditions imposed by man on his fellow man have resulted from the policy of SEGREGATION—*the setting apart of some from the flock*.

Minorities in every culture have suffered from policies of segregation. All through history, Jews have been confined to ghettos to segregate them from the mainstream. In the United States, segregation of Negroes was practiced extensively until most recently.

On May 17, 1954, in the case of Brown vs. the Topeka, Kansas, Board of Education, the Supreme Court of the United States made a historic ruling. It declared that segregated school systems, being "inherently unequal," are illegal. Statutes that prevented Negro children from attending public schools with white children were ruled to be a violation of the 14th Amendment of the Constitution. The "separate but equal" policy was thus shown up for the lie it was.

EGREGIOUS

Separated from the herd, outstanding, flagrant, remarkably bad.

He made an egregious mistake in overlooking one of his colleagues when he was making the introductions at the meeting.

GREGARIOUS

Friendly, sociable, fond of the company of others.

People who are described as extroverts are generally gregarious, and prefer doing things with others to being alone.

DESEGREGATION

The elimination of segregation.

Some cities are trying to achieve desegregation by busing youngsters to schools outside their own neighborhoods.

CONGREGATE

To come together in a group.

The membership of a church is usually called a congregation— a body of persons who assemble for worship.

AGGREGATE

Collected into one body, a total or whole.

In the aggregate, his debts amounted to $5,000.

HUMUS

Meaning: Soil, ground, vegetable mold.

Origin: Latin, *humus*, soil, ground, earth.

Notwithstanding man's recent ability to soar, man's most basic relationship is to the earth. Though he can now journey to the moon, man's roots are in the soil.

The relationship of man and the earth is clearly preserved linguistically. In Hebrew, the generic word for *man* is the same as the name of the first man, Adam; the Hebrew word for "earth" is "adam." In English, the word HUMAN comes from the root "humus," the Latin word for "soil."

POSTHUMOUS

Born after the father's death; published after the author's death.

Ernest Hemingway's last book, Islands in the Stream, *was published posthumously.*

HUMILIATE

To humble, to reduce someone's dignity, to drag him down to the ground; to hurt someone's pride or feelings.

The wise men have said, "He who humiliates a person in public has no share in the world to come."

HOMAGE

The acknowledgement of allegiance to another man.

In the Middle Ages, under the feudal system, lower-ranking knights would pay homage to higher nobility, swearing loyalty and military service to them.

Honor, reverence.

When President Roosevelt died, many people attended his funeral to pay homage to him.

HUMANE

Having the best qualities of mankind; kind, tender, merciful.

The Red Cross tries to see that prisoners of war are treated in a humane way.

HUMUS

Organic part of the soil, decayed leaves and vegetable matter used as fertilizer.

He added humus to the soil before planting his tomato seeds.

HUMAN

Pertaining to man, the earthly being.

There is a famous saying by Alexander Pope regarding the fallibility of human nature: "To err is human, to forgive divine."

HUMBLE

Modest, not proud; having a low opinion of oneself.

Although he was regarded as one of the greatest scholars of his time, the rabbi had a very humble manner.

IATRO

Meaning: A doctor, medical.

Origin: Greek, *iatros*, a doctor, physician.

For a very long time, the only diseases that were recognized were diseases of the body. Mental patients were regarded as subhuman. Then, in the twentieth century, doctors began to study the emotional basis of disease. PSYCHIATRISTS specialize in the treatment of disorders of the mind.

Sigmund Freud, the great explorer of the human mind, revealed that all of us have a vast area of the subconscious buried within our conscious minds. In the subconscious are gathered the memories of all the things that ever happened to us, especially in the early years of our lives. Every hurt, wound, slight, insult, every act of love and kindness shown to us—they are all there, powerfully and subconsciously influencing our every act in life.

Freud made a tremendous contribution to the theory and practice of psychiatry, to the understanding of human behavior, and to the treatment of mental disorders called *psychoses* and *neuroses*.

PEDIATRICIAN

A doctor specializing in the diseases of children.

When she described her child's symptoms to the pediatrician over the phone, he told her to bring the child to his office because he suspected the child had chicken pox.

GERIATRICS

The branch of medical science that deals with the health problems of old people.

His interest in old people led him to specialize in geriatrics.

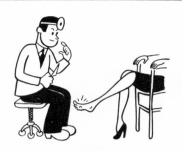

PODIATRIST

A doctor who specializes in the troubles of the feet.

When her bunions became so painful that she couldn't wear shoes, she went to the podiatrist to have them removed.

IT IR

Meaning: To go.

Origin: Latin, *ire*, to go.
Latin, *iter*, a walk, journey.

Did you ever wonder why the word OATH can imply both *reverence,* on the one hand, and *irreverence,* or *disrespect,* on the other? When you take an oath of office, or an oath of marriage, you solemnly promise to be honest and faithful. But sometimes, when you are angry, you use an oath, or *a swear-word.*

There is a simple connecting line between these two different meanings of the word OATH. The word is derived from the Latin root "ire," meaning *to go.* Originally, when you took an oath, you went on a journey to fulfill a promise, and you called on God to witness your promise.

Soon, people began to use the name of God whenever they felt strongly about something, thus, the oath, "I swear to God," could be meant literally, or it could be an expression of anger.

AMBIENCE

What is around; the surrounding atmosphere.

We always go to that restaurant because it is beautiful and quiet and we like the ambience.

EXIT

Where you go out.

On an airplane, the stewardess always points out the exits.

INITIAL

At the beginning.

The new athletic program was very disorganized in its initial stages.

The first letter of a word or name.

We gave Mary a gold bracelet with her initials on it.

INITIATE

To go into something for the first time, to begin, to introduce.

The employees were delighted when their company initiated a policy of sick leave.

To admit as a member.

Before he was initiated into the fraternity, he had to show he was a good sport by carrying out the initiation task of climbing the flagpole.

CIRCUIT

A going around.

On New Year's Eve the young couple made a circuit of all the nightclubs.

A path over which electrical current flows.

A fuse is a circuit breaker and cuts off electricity when the wires are overloaded.

SEDITION

Stirring up of rebellion against the government, going against.

It is difficult to judge whether a revolutionary speaker is guilty of sedition or whether he is exercising the right to free speech.

INITIATIVE

Readiness and ability to be the one to take the first step, to introduce new ideas or methods.

John has no initiative and always waits to be told exactly what to do

ISSUE

To give out.

The army issued uniforms to the new soldiers.

A question to be discussed.

The main issue in the strike was shorter working hours.

Something sent out.

The latest issue of the magazine has an article about pop art.

Offspring.

They were married for twenty years but had no issue.

TRANSITION

Going across, a change from one condition to another.

Many Arab states are trying to make the transition from a feudal, medieval life to that of the twentieth century.

REITERATE

To repeat, to go over something again and again.

The accused reiterated endlessly, "I did not do it."

OBITUARY

A notice detailing the life of someone who has died.

The obituary column of the newspaper tells of the lives and deeds of those who have died that day.

ITINERARY

A list of places where you will be going, a plan of a journey.

His itinerary included all the major countries of Western Europe.

AMBITIOUS

Going all-out in order to achieve success.

John is very smart, but he is not ambitious and does not strive to get ahead.

J E C T

Meaning: To throw.

Origin: Latin, *jacere*, to throw.

Once, the fear of poliomyelitis, or infantile paralysis, hung heavy in the hearts of all. One could see the results of this dread disease all about. Victims of polio were paralyzed, crippled, and sometimes died. No one, neither young nor old, rich nor poor, was exempt from the ravages of the disease.

Then, Jonas Salk, a doctor from New York, declared war on polio—and won. After years of experimenting, he created a vaccine that protected against the disease.

The doctor tells you to roll up your sleeve and get ready for the INJECTION. With a swift jab, he thrusts a needle into your skin. You may be uncomfortable for a little while, but that is a small price to pay for immunity.

PROJECTOR

A machine for throwing an image on a screen.

They bought a projector and now they show movies in their own home.

ADJECTIVE

A word that qualifies or limits a noun.

In the sentence "He is a wise king," the word wise *is an adjective.*

CONJECTURE

A thought or an idea that was thrown together.

Columbus' conjecture that the world was round did not lead him to India but to a discovery of momentous importance.

JET

A stream of fluid, air or gases gushing forth.

The firemen propelled a jet of water at the burning building.

JET

A stream of fluid, air or gases gushing forth.

A jet plane is propelled forward by the discharge of a jet of heated air and gases.

TRAJECTORY

The curved path of a body moved by force.

The night was moonless and dark, but the flame shooting from the rocket made its trajectory easy to follow.

REJECT

To throw back, to refuse to take, not to accept.

The army doctors rejected him because his eyesight was very poor.

EJECT

To throw out.

The noisy drunk was ejected from the barroom.

OBJECT

A material thing.

There was a strange-looking object in the box and no one could figure out what purpose it served.

The purpose, goal.

The object of the game is to get the ball into the hole with a minimum number of tries.

To oppose.

His parents did not object to his long hair.

Part of a sentence.

In the sentence "Mary hit John," John is the object.

SUBJECT

To throw or place under.

He teased her and subjected her to one torment after another.

A person under the power of another.

Mary is a relaxed person and makes a good subject for hypnotism.

Something studied.

His favorite school subject is math.

Subject of a sentence.

In the sentence "Mary hit John," Mary is the subject.

PROJECT

A design, a scheme, a proposal that has been set forth.

The students were constructing different models of homes for their social studies project.

To go forward.

Fortune tellers try to project into the future.

To stick out.

He projected his head from the window to call her.

JETTY

A landing pier.

A jetty enables a boat to dock and unload on dry land.

JUR JUS

Meaning: To swear, to be righteous.

Origin: Latin, *jus*, *juris*, law, right.
Latin, *jurare*, to take an oath, swear.

Man yearns for JUSTICE, for *fair treatment*. When his deeds are judged, man hopes to be dealt with JUSTLY.

A story is told in the Bible of the wicked cities of Sodom and Gomorrah. The cries of those who misbehaved and of those who were mistreated rose to the heavens.

The Lord God decided to destroy the wicked cities. He told the patriarch, Abraham, about his plan.

But Abraham protested: "Perhaps there are some righteous people in these cities. Would you sweep the innocent away with the guilty?"

And Abraham dared to bargain with God to spare the cities for the sake of the few who were innocent of evil, saying, "Shall not the Judge of all the world deal justly?"

JURISDICTION

The area in which authority or power is exercised.

The courts have jurisdiction not only over our own citizens but over foreigners who are living here as well.

PERJURE

To swear against the truth, to lie under oath

Although the policeman swore that he had not been involved in bribery, the marked bills were evidence that he had perjured himself.

JUDGE

An official who hears and decides cases in court.

The judge gave the accused man a suspended sentence and let him go.

A person with authority to pick the winner or settle an argument.

John was one of the judges for the poster contest.

To form an opinion about, to criticize.

The teacher felt he could not judge Mary's work because she had been absent so much.

INJURY

Unjust treatment; physical harm.

If you hit a man with your car and then yell at him and call him a fool, you would be adding insult to injury.

JUSTIFY

To show that something is fair; to free from blame.

Some people will commit illegal or indecent acts for a cause they believe in because they argue that the end justifies the means.

To supply good grounds for.

John tried to justify his poor grade on the exam by claiming that he hadn't been feeling well.

JUDICIOUS

Wise and careful.

He was judicious in selecting furniture so that his apartment could serve both as a home and an office.

PREJUDICE

Preconceived idea, opinion held before the facts are known; intolerance; bias.

Practices that exclude people of certain races, religions, or nationalities from jobs, schools, or housing are based · on the worst kind of prejudice.

CONJURE

To practice magic; to summon a demon or spirit by an oath or magic spell.

The magician conjured a rabbit out of his hat.

To cause to appear.

Although the poor woman was penniless, she managed to conjure up a meal of soup and vegetables for her hungry children.

JURY

A group of people who are sworn in to listen to the evidence and to bring in a just verdict.

The jury found him guilty of murder.

A group of experts who select the winners and award the prizes.

The jury awarded first prize in the beauty contest to a young woman from Australia.

L A T

Meaning: To carry.

Origin: Latin, *latus*, p.p. of *ferre*, to bring, to bear.

The word TRANSLATE means *to carry over from one language to another*.

There are between 3,000 and 4,000 languages spoken throughout the world. Most of us understand and speak only one language fluently. We depend on TRANSLATORS and TRANSLATIONS to communicate to us the words of cultures other than our own.

The first translation ever made was the translation of the Hebrew Bible into Greek, presumably at the request of Ptolemy Philadelphus, King of Egypt in 250 B.C. In 400 A.D., St. Jerome translated the Bible into Latin. This translation was called the *Vulgate*. The Bible has now been translated into 1200 languages.

Some words have become so universal, they need no translation. One example is the Hebrew word, AMEN, which means *may this prayer come true*. The translators of the Bible liked this Hebrew word and always carried it over without change into their translations.

RELATIVE

A kinsman, a person related by blood.

All the relatives get together about once a year for a wedding or a funeral.

Compared to something else.

Relative to his limited experience, he was making a good salary.

CORRELATE

To show the relation between two things.

Science has shown that heavy smoking is correlated with lung cancer.

COLLATE

To compare, to put side by side .

The students mimeographed 100 copies of each of the four pages of the story and then collated all the sets.

RELATE

To give an account of, to carry back.

Our friend who served in Viet Nam related his experiences to us.

To connect, to show an association between.

The eye doctor said that the child's reading difficulties were related to a vision problem.

ELATED

In high spirits, joyful.

The author was elated because a publisher had accepted his manuscript.

PRELATE

A high ranking church dignitary.

When there is an election of a new Pope, the prelates of the Catholic Church gather in Rome.

LEG   LECT

Meaning: To choose, to pick, to read.

Origin: Latin, *legere*, to choose, to read.

In English, it is very common for a word to have several disparate meanings. For example, to STRIKE can mean *to hit,* or it can mean *to refuse to work;* a BALL may be something to play with, or it may be a fancy social dance. In Latin, too, a word may have rather different and unrelated meanings. The Latin word "legere," for example, means *to pick or choose,* and it also means *to read.*

When man first began to record language, pictures were used instead of words. Little by little, the pictures became more and more abstract. Eventually, the alphabet was invented.

Then visual symbols were selected, not to represent a whole word, but to correspond to each sound within the word. When a written language is highly phonetic, each written symbol (or letter) represents a sound. When you read, you are, in effect, selecting the sound that goes with the letter.

LEGIBLE

Readable.

He learned little from her letters because her handwriting was not very legible.

ELIGIBLE

Qualified to be chosen.

As a war veteran he was eligible for a special pension.

ELITE

The best people; the choice part of a group.

The college has an excellent athletic reputation and its basketball players are the campus elite.

LEGEND

A story that has come down from the distant past.

He spent his vacation reading the exciting legends of King Arthur.

LECTURE

A speech on a chosen subject.

The professor's lecture was so boring that half the class fell asleep.

LECTURE

A scolding.

Johnny's mother always lectures him about keeping his room neat.

SELECT

To choose.

Mary was very proud to be selected for the school play.

Superior, outstanding.

The members of Arista are selected on the basis of grades and form a select group of students.

COLLECT, COLLECTION

Gather together, accumulate.

My mother collects china cups and saucers as a hobby.

Get payment.

The students collected money for a present for their teacher who was leaving to have a baby.

ELECT

To choose or pick out by vote.

The President of the United States is elected for a four-year term.

LEGION

An army; a large number.

The soldiers of the Roman legion were picked for their strength and bravery.

COLLEAGUE

A fellow worker, one chosen at the same time.

The history teacher disagreed with his colleagues about the school's policy on students who cut class.

ELEGANT

Showing richness or refinement of taste.

She chose an elegant gown for the wedding.

L E G

Meaning: Law.

Origin: Latin, *lex*, *legis*, law.

Whenever people gather together to live in groups, they formulate rules of conduct to guide their behavior. The set of rules that dictates what may or may not be done is the LAW.

No matter how simple or complex his society, man has always lived by a code of law. Of course, the law differs from one society to another. The law of each society reflects the most important ethical and religious concepts of the people. One of the most important aspects of the law is its adaptability; it grows and changes to conform to the needs of the people.

The earliest systems of law known to us are the Babylonian Code of Hammurabi, the Indian Laws of Manu, and the Mosaic Law of the Hebrews of ancient Palestine. These have influenced and informed the spirit of our modern law.

Modern law also owes much to the Justinian codification of Roman law. Later, the Napoleonic Code formed the basis for modern civil law. The concepts of Sir William Blackstone regarding the natural rights of man also influenced the law of the United States.

LEGISLATURE

The body of persons responsible for making the laws.

The legislature of the United States, called the Congress, is composed of the Senate and the House of Representatives.

ILLEGITIMATE

Not lawful; born out of wedlock.

The widespread use of birth control and abortion has reduced the number of illegitimate births.

LEGAL

Permitted by law.

In some schools it is still legal for a teacher to use corporal punishment.

ILLEGAL

Not lawful.

A noted wit complained: "Everything I like is illegal, immoral, or fattening."

PRIVILEGE

A right; a special advantage or favor enjoyed by some.

Senior citizens may apply for cards which will give them the privilege of reduced rates for certain things.

LEGITIMATE

Lawful, proper.

He had a doctor's note to show he had a legitimate reason for being absent from school.

LEGISLATE

To pass laws.

The mayor wanted the council to legislate against gambling.

LITH

Meaning: Stone.

Origin: Greek, *lithos*, stone.

There was a time, about a million years ago, when there were no tools and few weapons. This era is known as the PALEOLITHIC period, or Old Stone Age. It is the earliest and longest period in mankind's history.

During the Old Stone Age, man lived in a hostile environment. Strange and terrible beasts abounded. The only weapons man had to combat his enemies were sticks, stones, and his bare hands.

Then man began to chip one stone with a harder stone. Soon someone discovered that shaping a handle on a stone gave a weapon a crushing power. Weapons became more varied and more refined.

In the NEOLITHIC period, or New Stone Age, men sharpened, ground, polished, and perfected their stone weapons and tools until they were highly efficient instruments.

The most important achievements of this period, however, were farming and the domestication of animals. These discoveries enabled man to make the transition from a nomadic existence dependent on hunting to a more settled life in villages and cities.

MONOLITH

A single block or pillar of stone.

The monument in honor of George Washington in Washington, D. C., is a monolith.

MONOLITHIC

Massively solid and uniform.

Americans value diversity in ideas and life style and are suspicious of the monolithic nature of culture and society in totalitarian regimes.

LITHOGRAPHY

Printing from a flat stone or metal plate.

Lithography is a process used both by fine artists and by commercial offset printers to produce many copies of a work.

LOGOS

Meaning: Speech, *a description or a science of.*

Origin: Greek, *logos*, speech, a word.

There are about 300 English words which end in the suffix *ology,* and the number increases as the frontiers of our knowledge expand. The suffix *ology* indicates a branch of thought or science. As new discoveries and concepts are developed, new words have to be coined.

It is a common practice to borrow and combine foreign roots, prefixes, and suffixes to describe a new idea or product. Here are a few examples of some new "ologies":

EPIDEMIOLOGY is a special branch of medical science that deals with epidemics—contagious diseases that spread rapidly. A doctor skilled in this field is called an EPIDEMIOLOGIST.

Another important new science is IMMUNOLOGY—the branch of medical science that deals with how the body develops and maintains immunity, or freedom from contagion.

EPILOGUE

Words spoken after.

There was an epilogue at the end of the movie that told what happend to the people on whom the movie was based.

LOGARITHM

A system of using exponents to shorten mathematical calculations.

The logarithm of 1,000 is 3.

EULOGY

Beautiful words spoken in praise, most often at a funeral.

One of the most famous eulogies is the Gettysburg Address, spoken by Abraham Lincoln in 1863 at the dedication of the national cemetery at the Civil War battlefield of Gettysburg.

SYLLOGISM

A form of reasoning in which a logical conclusion is drawn from two statements.

An example of a syllogism would be: All men are mortal. Socrates is a man. Therefore Socrates is mortal.

PSYCHOLOGY

The study of the human mind the science of human and animal behavior.

He decided to study child psychology, because he was fascinated with the way children develop.

MONOLOGUE

A long speech by one person.

John is a poor listener and a conversation with him usually turns into a monologue with John doing all the talking.

LOGIC

The science of forms of thinking; correct reasoning.

He did not use logic in fixing up his new apartment and painted himself into a corner.

PROLOGUE

A preface or introduction.

In his prologue, the author will generally tell why he wrote the book.

BIOLOGY

The study of living things.

John had to study the names of all the bones of the head for his biology test.

DIALOGUE

A talk or conversation between two persons.

The plot of the play was very interesting, but the dialogue was flat and unconvincing.

L O Q U I

Meaning: To speak

Origin: Latin, *loqui*, to speak.

My Fair Lady is a musical that has captivated audiences all over the world. Based on *Pygmalion,* a play by George Bernard Shaw, this delightful theatrical entertainment conveys an important message: people are known and judged by their manner of speaking.

In his exuberant comedy, Shaw, a vigorous enemy of social evil, launched a combined campaign against poverty and against phonetic abuse. Believing that the speech of the poor perpetuates social stratification, he has Eliza Doolittle come to Professor Henry Higgins for ELOCUTION lessons to improve her manner of speech. By changing her atrocious vowels and consonants to proper speech elements, the famous phonetician transforms the street urchin into a lady, and successfully passes her off in high society.

COLLOQUIAL

Used in informal, everyday conversation.

Many idioms and colloquial expressions add color to spoken language but are avoided in formal communication.

LOQUACIOUS

Very talkative.

He was usually rather shy and quiet at parties, but having a cocktail made him loquacious.

ELOQUENT

Beautifully expressive, speaking so as to stir the emotions.

He made a very eloquent speech in favor of continuing open enrollment in college.

SOLILOQUY

Talking to oneself.

The famous line "To be or not to be, that is the question" is from Hamlet's soliloquy.

VENTRILOQUIST

An entertainer who can project his voice so that it seems to come from another source.

The ventriloquist entertained the children by making it appear that the dog was talking.

MANIA

Meaning: An excessive or abnormal craving, an obsession, craze.

Origin: Greek, *mania*, madness

Until only recently, human madness was little understood. The emotionally ill were regarded with fear and mistrust. Too often, they were treated as raving MANIACS or lunatics. Mental institutions were worse than prisons, and patients were outrageously abused.

Early reformers, such as Dorothea Dix, fought for legislation to improve these deplorable conditions. Today, much progress has been made in the diagnosis and treatment of the mentally ill.

PYROMANIA

A compulsion to set fires.

Pyromaniacs are responsible for the destruction of millions of dollars worth of property each year.

BIBLIOMANIA

A passion for acquiring books.

His passion for old books had become bibliomania, and his home was more like a bookshop.

DIPSOMANIA

Insatiable desire for alcohol.

The Alcoholics Anonymous organization has been successful in relieving some people of the disease of dipsomania.

MEGALOMANIA

Suffering from delusions of grandeur, importance, and general godliness.

Not all megalomaniacs are in mental hospitals; many of them are in high offices in government.

KLEPTOMANIA

Compulsion to steal.

Although she had enough money to buy whatever she wanted, she suffered from kleptomania and would constantly steal things from stores.

MANUS

Meaning: Hand.

Origin: Latin, *manus*, hand.

Until the mid-fifteenth century, all knowledge was handed down in the form of MANUSCRIPTS, handwritten documents. In the monasteries, monks laboriously copied down the wisdom of the previous ages for future generations.

Illuminated manuscripts were also a great art form. Many of surpassing beauty can be seen in museums today.

An astounding discovery was made in the late 1940's. Hundreds of fragments and some fairly complete original works of the Bible and other ancient writings were found in caves near the Dead Sea, where they were preserved by the extremely dry air. These manuscripts, written between the first century B.C. and the first century A.D., are called the *Dead Sea Scrolls*. They are among the oldest readable manuscripts that we have.

The invention of printing from movable type is attributed to Johann Gutenberg. The famous Gutenberg, or Mazarin, Bible printed at Mainz, Germany, around 1456, was the first book printed from movable type.

Today, when you submit a manuscript to a publisher you would not dream of writing it by hand. With the invention of the typewriter and modern printing techniques, the word MANUSCRIPT has lost its literal meaning.

MANICURE

Care of the hands.

She goes to the beauty parlor every two weeks to have her nails manicured.

MANDATORY

Required, obligatory.

It is mandatory to declare all your earnings on your income tax return.

MANUAL

By hand.

Modern electrical appliances have practically eliminated manual labor in the kitchen.

MANUAL

A handbook.

John constructed his own hi-fi set by following the directions in the manual.

MANUFACTURE

To make.

The company manufactures all kinds of paper products.

To make up.

John didn't want to tell his mother how his pants tore, so he manufactured a story.

MANNER

Personal or social behavior.

It is considered bad manners to stare at people.

The way something is done.

Mary prepared the dinner in her own manner, ignoring her aunt's instructions.

MANACLE

A handcuff, shackle.

The prisoner's ability to work was limited by the manacles on his wrists.

MANIPULATE

To handle skillfully.

Although one engine broke down, the pilot manipulated the controls of the plane so that it did not crash.

To influence in an unfair way.

While washing the dishes, the wife felt she had been manipulated by her husband's pleas of overwork and fatigue.

MAINTAIN

To hold on, to keep.

The two candidates maintained friendly relations in spite of their differences.

To declare to be true.

The salesman maintained that his product was the best one on the market.

RECOMMEND

To speak in favor of.

Mary's former employer recommended her highly.

To advise.

John's instructor recommended that he take additional driving lessons.

COMMAND

To give an order; to require.

The Ten Commandments form the basis of Christian ethics.

To deserve and get.

The professor commands great respect from both students and colleagues for his vast knowledge.

COMMEND

To put in the care of another.

When his father died, the child was commended to the care of his uncle.

To praise.

The teacher commended John for the research he did for his report.

MANDATE

To put into one's hands; an order; clear instructions; authorization.

John was given a mandate to direct the basketball team whenever the coach was absent.

MANAGE

To have charge of.

*He managed the business
efficiently and the workers
justly.*

To handle, control.

*The baby sitter could not
manage the child.*

To bring about, to arrange.

*Mary managed to get all her
work done early so she could
be free for the weekend.*

MEN MIN

Meaning: To use one's mind, to think, to remember.

Origin: Latin, *mens*, *mentis*, the mind.
Greek, *mnasthai*, to use one's mind, to remember.

The exalted origin of the word MAN is clear in the plural form, *men*, from *mental*. It is inspiring to note that man was so named because he was *the one that thinks*.

If you have ever seen a copy—the original is in Paris—of the famous sculpture by Auguste Rodin called *The Thinker*, you would agree that the essential nature of man stems from his ability to think.

MENTALITY

The power of thinking.

Although he was only seven years old, he had the mentality of an adult.

REMIND

To call to mind, to cause to remember.

His mother always has to remind him to take his eyeglasses to school.

MEMORY

The power of remembering.

Mary has a poor memory and often forgets her own telephone number.

What is remembered.

Psychologists tell us that we often bury memories of unpleasant experiences.

In remembrance of.

John lit a candle in memory of his grandfather.

REMEMBER

Think of again.

John was worried because he could not remember whether he had locked the car doors.

Keep in mind.

Grandmother always remembers the children's birthdays.

To give regards.

The professor asked me to remember him to my father.

MIND

Mental powers, memory.

John couldn't concentrate on his schoolwork because he had other things on his mind.

Obey.

The students refused to mind the substitute teacher.

Feel concern about.

Mary doesn't mind if her sister borrows her clothes.

MENTAL

Of the mind, in one's head.

He made a mental note of each person's name as he was introduced.

MENTION

To bring to mind, to refer to.

He mentioned his experience in tutoring when he applied for a teaching job.

DEMENTED

Out of one's mind, insane.

After years of solitary confinement, the prisoner became demented.

MEMENTO

Something that helps you remember.

He saved the ticket stubs as a memento of their trip together.

COMMENT

A short statement of what you think; to remark.

The teacher asked for questions and comments about the lecture.

MEMORANDUM

A short note to help you remember.

After the meeting, he wrote a memorandum of the major points that were discussed.

AMNESTY

Pardon, not to remember.

One of the issues in the American Presidential election was whether to grant amnesty to the men who had evaded the Viet Nam draft.

REMINISCE

Call back to one's mind.

At the camp reunion, they spent most of the time reminiscing about the summer.

AMNESIA

Not remembering, loss of memory.

As a result of the automobile accident, he suffered from amnesia and did not know who he was.

MEMORIAL

Something that is a reminder.

At the end of the religious service, they recited a short memorial prayer in honor of the dead.

COMMEMORATE

To call to remembrance; to mark by some ceremony or observation.

To commemorate their twenty-fifth wedding anniversary, they took a second honeymoon.

METER

Meaning: Measure.

Origin: Greek, *metron*, measure.

People in England and America have a rather complicated series of weights and measures. Inches, feet, and miles are used to measure distance. Ounces, pounds, and tons are used to measure weight.

The rest of the world uses what is called the METRIC system, in which everything is calculated by tens, hundreds, and thousands. The metric system, is very simple, and highly scientific. Although our changeover to the metric system will be difficult and costly, it seems clear that such a change is inevitable, and will be worthwhile.

There are literally hundreds of words ending in *meter*. Each of these words describes something that is to be measured.

PERIMETER

The measure around the outer boundary of an area.

A picket fence went all around the perimeter of the field.

DIAMETRIC

Exactly opposite.

They managed to remain good friends even though their political views were diametrically opposed.

PROMISE

Send forth your word that you will do something, vow.

He promised his girlfriend that he would marry her.

DIAMETER

The measure of the length of a straight line from one side of a circle to the other passing through the center.

The diameter of the water hose was one inch.

TRIGONOMETRY

A branch of mathematics dealing with the measurement of triangles.

Trigonometry originated in Egypt where land measurements were very important because of the annual flooding of the Nile.

SYMMETRY

The state which exists when parts are harmoniously put together, equally balanced on opposite sides of a line.

Home decorators often avoid using symmetry in grouping pieces of furniture because the result is usually dull.

COMMENSURATE

Equal in measure, proportionate.

He felt his salary was not commensurate with the work he performed and he asked for a raise.

SPEEDOMETER

An instrument that measures the speed of the car.

When he saw the police car on the side of the road, he watched his speedometer to be sure he was driving within the speed limit.

KILOMETER

A thousand meters.

A kilometer is equivalent to ⅔ of a mile.

BAROMETER

An instrument for measuring the pressure of the atmosphere, used in forecasting the weather.

When the barometer falls sharply, we know there is a storm coming up.

THERMOMETER

An instrument which measures heat.

When her child was very cranky, the mother took his temperature, and the thermometer showed that he had a fever.

MIT   MIS

Meaning: To send.

Origin: Latin, *mittere*, to send.

As Marshall McLuhan pointed out, modern media of communication have reduced the world to a global village. Years ago, the peoples of the world were isolated from one another. But today, we have the ability to instantly transmit news and information all over the world.

The words in this family differ greatly in their meanings. However, they all deal with something that is sent. What it *is* that is sent may differ crucially, as illustrated by the two words MISSILE and MISSIONARY. One is sent on a mission of death, and the other goes forth on a mission of life.

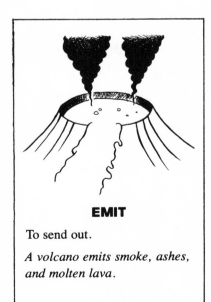

EMIT

To send out.

A volcano emits smoke, ashes, and molten lava.

EMIT

To utter.

The puppy emitted small whimpering sounds when he was left alone in the house.

COMMITTEE

A group of people within an organization who are assigned a particular function.

A committee was appointed to study the lunchroom situation and make suggestions for improving it.

MISSIONARY

A person sent out by the church to preach in a foreign country.

The missionaries in Africa often did as much to improve health and education conditions as they did to spread the Christian religion.

ADMISSION

Right of entry, entrance fee.

The seniors charged one dollar for admission to their show in order to raise money for their prom.

Confession.

Johnny made a frank admission about the part he had played in the student riot.

SUBMIT

To place oneself under the control of another, to yield, to surrender.

When their food and ammunition were all gone, the soldiers were forced to submit to the enemy.

To suggest, to propose.

Mary submitted her poem to the student newspaper.

TRANSMIT

To send across.

The sun transmits heat and light to the earth.

To hand down, to communicate.

He transmitted his love of music to his children.

MISSILE

Military weapon, rocket.

The United States and the Soviet Union have been trying to negotiate an agreement about controls in the military use of intercontinental ballistic missiles (ICBM).

PERMIT

A written warrant or license.

You cannot get into an atomic research station without a special permit.

To allow.

The teacher permitted the children to choose whatever books they wanted.

ADMIT

To let in.

The windows were small and did not admit enough light and air.

To confess.

The teacher admitted that the test was very hard.

COMMISSION

Authorization to perform certain duties.

He was given a commission to investigate bribery in the police force.

Military rank.

The sergeant distinguished himself in battle and was given a commission as a lieutenant.

REMIT

To send back; to pay.

His bill was long overdue and he received a letter asking him to please remit at once.

To pardon, cancel.

The prisoner was delighted when the judge remitted his sentence.

REMISS

Careless, negligent in performing a job.

The husband complained that his wife was remiss about keeping track of her expenditures.

COMMIT

To entrust, to promise, to place with another for safety.

When his brother died, he committed himself to supporting his nieces and nephews.

To put in confinement; to do something wrong.

He was committed to jail for committing a robbery.

MESSAGE

A communication sent from one to another.

His job during the war was to decode messages intercepted by the secret service.

MESSENGER

A person who delivers messages or packages.

During the summer, the student got a job as a Western Union messenger.

MON   MONIT

Meaning: To warn, to remind.

Origin: Latin, *monere*, to warn, to remind.
Latin, *moneta*, a mint.

We now come to the root of all evil—money. Isn't it curious that the word MONEY comes from the root which means *to warn, to remind.* There is an interesting story in Roman mythology that demonstrates how this came about.

The Roman goddess Juno was the wife of Jupiter and the queen of the gods. One of her duties was to warn the Romans of any danger coming upon them. The full name of this Roman goddess was Juno Moneta.

Now it so happened that in the temple of Juno Moneta there was a workshop for making coins, which was called the MINT. Likewise, the coins that were made were called MONEY—after Juno Moneta.

MONITOR

An advisor, a warner; a student chosen to help the teacher.

The monitor was unable to control the class in the teacher's absence.

MONITOR

To check transmission of radio and TV broadcasts.

John monitored the TV program and gave the cameramen some useful suggestions.

PREMONITION

A feeling that something will happen, a foreboding.

Alone on a dark, deserted street, he had a premonition of danger.

MONEY

Any medium of exchange, wealth.

Although money can't buy happiness, having money does make people feel secure.

MINT

A place where money is coined.

The United States mint is reissuing the two dollar bill.

A large amount.

John's new car must have cost him a mint.

SUMMON

To call with authority to some duty, to send for.

The police summoned all the suspects in the murder to appear in court.

To call forth.

Mary summoned up her last bit of strength to lift her grandmother onto the bed.

ADMONISH

To warn.

The teacher admonished the pupils to work independently and not copy from each other.

To call someone down, to rebuke.

The principal admonished the student for cutting class.

MONUMENTAL

Notable, important.

His book on the history of trade unionism was a monumental work of research.

Huge.

Mary showed a monumental ignorance of classical music.

MONUMENT

Something set up to remind us of a person or event.

Designed by Henry Bacon like a Greek temple, the Lincoln Monument, with its magnificent statue of Lincoln by Daniel Chester French, stands in Potomac Park, Washington, D. C.

M O R   M O R T

Meaning: To die.

Origin: Latin, *mors*, *mortis*, to die.

The central, inescapable fact of life is the inevitability of death. Man is the only living creature who faces life with the conscious awareness that he is mortal and must die.

The Latin phrase *rigor mortis* graphically describes the inelegant stiffening of the muscles that occurs several hours after death.

Man has always cherished a persistent, passionate hope that somehow death is not the end of life—that the soul lives on in some future existence. In almost every religion, there is a concept of resurrection, of a paradise that awaits man after death.

MORTGAGE

A document which gives a lender a claim to property if the debt is not paid.

He didn't have much cash and was only able to buy the house because he got a government-subsidized mortgage.

MORIBUND

About to die, coming to an end.

Polygamy was at one time a widespread institution throughout the world, but it can now be said to be moribund.

AMORTIZE

To gradually pay off (or kill) a debt.

As a homeowner amortizes his mortgage, he has more and more of a feeling of owning his home.

IMMORTAL

Lasting forever.

Of all the people who have lived on this earth, only a few have achieved immortal fame for their contributions in the arts, sciences, or history.

MORTICIAN

The man who arranges for the burial of the dead, undertaker.

The mortician made all the arrangements for the funeral.

MORTIFY

To humiliate, to vex severely.

Mary was mortified when she forgot her lines in the middle of the performance.

MORTALITY

Death, the death rate.

Modern medical practice has decreased infant mortality all over the world.

MORTAL

A human being, who must eventually die.

The ancient Roman writer Seneca is responsible for the famous line, "What fools these mortals be."

Causing death.

John's ego received a mortal blow when he was turned down by the college he had applied to.

POST-MORTEM

An examination of a body after death.

When someone dies under suspicious circumstances, there is usually a post-mortem.

An examination of an issue after it has been resolved.

Many people engage in useless post-mortem discussions.

MURDER

To cause to die, to kill.

"Thou shalt not murder" is one of the Ten Commandments.

M O V   M O B   M O T

Meaning: To move.

Origin: Latin, *movere*, to move.

In 1861, in a village in Pennsylvania, a peculiar, heavy, dirty sort of water started bubbling fiercely out of a hole in the ground. Only it wasn't water—it was oil. This combustible substance, the result of the direct heat that the sun had poured on the earth in ages long past, is a gigantic source of energy. Coal also contains this heat, but in solid form.

Shortly after the discovery of oil came the discovery of an engine that could burn oil for fuel. It was called the internal combustion engine. About 80 years ago, this engine was placed in a wheeled carriage, and thus became the ancestor of our modern AUTOMOBILE.

Until the second decade of this century, carriages drawn by horses were universal. Today, most children never see a horse-drawn wagon or carriage except in a museum. The automobile, a self-propelled vehicle, has revolutionized transportation all over the world.

PROMOTE

To move forward.

Mary was rewarded for her excellent work as a teacher by being promoted to supervisor.

To stir up interest in something.

The company launched a program of advertising to promote their new product.

MOVEMENT

Motion, action.

John made a sudden movement which startled the dog and made him bark ferociously.

Organized activities by a group; trend.

After giving it much thought, Mary decided to join the Women's Lib movement.

MOBILE

Easily moved.

Many Americans live in mobile homes attached to vehicles in which they travel from place to place.

MOBILE

A form of sculpture that moves.

The American sculptor Alexander Calder invented the now famous mobile, consisting of abstract shapes suspended on wires.

DEMOTE

To move down, to reduce in rank.

The sergeant was demoted in rank for contradicting his officer's orders.

LOCOMOTIVE

An engine on wheels which moves a railroad train.

George Stephenson, an English engineer, built the first steam locomotive in 1815.

MOBILIZATION

The gathering up and moving of the Armed Forces to critical military points.

The Third Fleet practices mobilization so that it will be prepared in an emergency.

REMOVE

To move from the place
occupied; to take off.

*You must remove your shoes
before entering a Moslem
temple.*

REMOTE

Far removed; far off, distant in
time, place or manner.

*It is possible that in the remote
future man will conquer
disease.*

EMOTION

A strong feeling of joy,
sorrow, fear, hate, love, anger.

*As he witnessed the birth of his
first child, he was filled with
emotion.*

COMMOTION

Confusion, disturbance, agita-
tion.

*The announcement that every-
body had to vacate the
building because of fire caused
a great commotion.*

MOTION

Movement.

*Passengers are requested not
to talk to the driver while the
bus in in motion.*

A suggestion.

*Someone made a motion to
adjourn the meeting.*

MOTIVE

What moves one to action;
incentive, goal.

*Nobody could figure out the
motive for the murder.*

NOMOS

Meaning: Management, usage, order, arrangement.

Origin: Greek, *nemein*, to distribute, arrange.

In ancient Greece, the word ECONOMY had to do with the management of the income and expenditures of a household. The Latin root pertained to the management of a village, thus extending the meaning somewhat.

As the world's population increases and societies become larger and more complex, the management of economic affairs becomes more crucial. Today, ECONOMICS is a complicated science dealing with the production, consumption, and distribution of a nation's wealth. ECONOMISTS are very important people who advise and determine governmental policy in the areas of employment, taxation, finance, and social welfare.

The works of outstanding economists, such as *The Wealth of Nations* by Adam Smith (1776), and *The General Theory of Employment* by John Maynard Keynes (1936) continue to influence political thought and action.

AUTONOMY

The power to rule oneself, self-government.

Although the American colonies did have a certain measure of autonomy, they eventually desired complete independence from England.

NEMESIS

The goddess of just retribution; hence, an act of retributive justice; an inevitable result.

If John continues to ignore his homework assignments, he will face his nemesis at the final examination.

ASTRONOMY

The study of the stars, their order and arrangement.

The telescope is the most important piece of equipment used in astronomy.

METRONOME

A clocklike device with a pendulum that beats time.

The music teacher used a metronome to help his pupils in their piano practice.

ECONOMICAL

Not wasteful; thrifty.

It is usually more economical to buy canned and packaged goods in large quantities.

ONOMA

Meaning: A name.

Origin: Greek, *onoma*, a name.

Imagine a time many thousands of years ago. A man comes running out of the forest, breathless, wild-eyed, white with fear. He has just seen a lion in the woods and heard its deep-throated roar; he has barely escaped its ferocious claws. Now in the village, the man wants to tell his friends of the danger that lurks in the forest. So he screams out to them, imitating the lion's roar: *"ri--ri--ri!"* They hear and they understand.

The man has invented the word *roar*.

Picture little children playing at the edge of a clearing in front of their home. Suddenly their mother spots a snake approaching them, poised to strike. Horror-stricken, she *hisses* out to them a sharp warning sound: *"Ssssss!"* The children understand and run to safety.

These are two examples of ONOMATOPOEIC words; that is, *words formed by imitating natural sounds*. "Onoma" means a *name* or a *word,* and "poiein" is a Greek word meaning *to make*.

SYNONYM

A word having the same meaning as another.

English has a large number of synonyms because it borrowed words from different languages; e.g. regal (from the Latin), royal (from the French), and kingly (old English) are synonyms.

PSEUDONYM

A false or assumed name.

Mary Ann Evans was a great and talented 19th-century English novelist who wrote under the pseudonym of George Eliot because she felt that her novels would sell better if people thought they were written by a man.

HOMONYM

A word with the same sound as another but with a different meaning and spelling.

Find the homonyms in this sentence: The child was frightened when he saw the bear bare his teeth.

METONYMY

Naming something after one of its attributes; using the name of one thing for another that is associated with it.

An example of metonymy is the phrase "bed and board," meaning room and meals, the board signifying the table on which the food is served and the bed signifying the room.

ACRONYM

A word formed from the first letters of several words.

Army slang has given us some colorful acronyms, such as SNAFU (situation normal, all fouled up) and AWOL (absent without official leave).

ANTONYMS

Words whose meanings are opposite.

Many nursery rhymes make use of antonyms, e.g.: Pease porridge hot, Pease porridge cold; or Jack Sprat could eat no fat, his wife could eat no lean.

IGNOMINY

Dishonor, disgrace, shame; loss of name or reputation.

The mother suffered great ignominy when her son was convicted of robbery.

ANONYMOUS

Without a name.

Often, people who give money for charitable purposes prefer to remain anonymous.

PATRONYMIC

Name derived from the name of a father or ancestor.

Patronymic names are to be found in every language, e.g. Johnson, O'Brien, Ivanovich, MacDonald, Goldensohn, Ben Avi.

ORTHO

Meaning: Straight, *true, correct.*

Origin: Greek, *orthos,* straight.

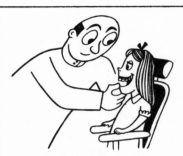

ORTHODONTIA

Straightening the teeth.

The child was undergoing orthodontia and had a mouthful of braces.

ORTHOPEDIST

A doctor who specializes in the treatment of bone ailments; orthopedists used to treat the bones of young children primarily, but today, of course, they treat patients of all ages.

Orthopedists are kept very busy straightening out broken limbs during the skiing season.

ORTHODOX

Proper, correct, conventional; conforming to established religious beliefs and doctrines.

Mary's ideas about sex are orthodox, and she was shocked to hear that the couple was living together without being married.

ORTHOGRAPHY

Spelling.

Judging by the frequency of spelling errors in students' compositions, orthography would seem to be a neglected subject.

PASS PATH

Meaning: To feel.

Origin: Greek, *pathos*, feeling, suffering.
Latin, *pati*, to suffer, to endure.

The human being is endowed with an exquisite nervous system that monitors and controls his adjustment to his environment. Part of this network is the autonomic nervous system which regulates involuntary responses. In this network, the SYMPATHETIC and the PARASYMPATHETIC systems operate in perfect balance. Thus it happens that sometimes, when these nerves respond sympathetically to each other, you may report a pain in one area of your body to your doctor and he may find the source of the trouble in a different area.

To repond SYMPATHETICALLY to another human being is to feel or endure his suffering as if it were your own. It is, perhaps, the ultimate human response.

ANTIPATHY

A feeling against, a strong dislike or aversion.

Many people have an antipathy to snakes.

IMPASSIVE

Not feeling or showing emotion.

No matter how hard the performers tried, the audience remained impassive.

OSTEOPATH

A person who treats certain bone and nerve ailments by manipulation.

Although many people think that osteopaths are frauds, John always goes to one when he has back trouble.

PSYCHOPATH

A disturbed person who cannot make moral judgments.

Rehabilitation programs are not usually effective with criminals who are psychopaths.

PATHETIC

Exciting pity or sadness.

The pathetic cry of the lost child brought many people to his assistance.

EMPATHY

The power of understanding the feelings and mind of another.

The need for empathy is expressed in the saying, "Do not judge a man until you are in his place."

COMPASSION

Sorrow for the trouble or suffering of others.

Mary was filled with compassion when she read about the victims of the famine.

PATHOLOGY

The study of disease; deviation from the normal state.

Doctors who search for germs through microscopes must be experts in pathology.

APATHY

Without feeling, lack of interest, indifference.

The public showed great apathy about the election, and not many people bothered to vote.

PASSIVE

Submissive, inactive, taking no part.

Mahatma Gandhi tried to bring about peaceful social and political reform by using fasting and other forms of passive resistance.

PASSION

Strong love; intense emotion.

Mary had a passion for the Rolling Stones and bought every one of their records.

PATIENCE

Ability to endure; ability to wait calmly.

Everyone admired the prospective father's patience as he calmly awaited the birth of his child.

PATHOS

A quality that arouses pity or sympathy.

The story about the old man and his dog was full of pathos.

P E D

Meaning: A child; a foot.

Origin: Greek, *paedos*, a child.
Latin, *pedis*, a foot.

There is something curious about this word root. Sometimes it means *a foot,* and at other times—confusingly enough—it means *a child*. The explanation is quite simple. English has taken over the Latin root "ped," meaning *a foot* and it has also taken over the Greek word "paedos," *a child*.

Perhaps because it was so eclectic, the English language contains more words than any other language. And the total number keeps growing. When Samuel Johnson published his great English dictionary in 1755, there were 150,000 entries. Modern dictionaries contain about 600,000 entries. It is estimated that in everyday speech we use about 60,000 different words.

In the following words, the root *ped* means foot:

PEDESTRIAN

One who goes on foot.

The car stopped in the middle of the street to let the pedestrian cross.

Slow or dull, lacking imagination.

The author's writing style was very boring, and his book on the drug problem was pedestrian.

EXPEDIENT

A means of extricating one's foot from a snare; based on what is useful in bringing about a desired result rather than on what is right or just.

After he had locked the keys in the car, the only expedient solution was to break the car window.

CENTIPEDE

A small wormlike animal with a pair of legs for each body segment.

Centipedes are harmful not because they have so many legs, but because their two front legs are poison fangs.

PEDESTAL

Base supporting a column, statue or lamp.

A bust of the founder of the school stood on a simple pedestal in the main hallway.

EXPEDITION

A setting forth on a voyage or journey, originally, marching on foot.

The first expedition which landed a man on the moon was a phenomenal scientific event.

PEDIGREE

Family tree, ancestry.

They bought a black poodle with a pedigree a mile long.

PEDAL

A lever operated by the foot; the operation of such a lever.

It was very difficult to pedal the bicycle uphill.

IMPEDIMENT

A hindrance, an obstacle.

When you are traveling in a foreign country, not knowing the language is a great impediment.

IMPEDE

To hinder, to obstruct, to hold the feet in.

He did not allow his illness to impede him from completing his studies in time to graduate.

EXPEDITE

To free someone who is, so to speak, caught by the feet; hence, to speed up, to hasten, to facilitate.

He was very anxious for the gift to reach her on her birthday, so he asked the store to expedite its delivery.

In the following words, the root *ped* means child:

PEDIATRICIAN

A doctor who specializes in the care and treatment of children.

The office of the pediatrician was crammed with children and their anxious mothers.

ORTHOPEDIST

A doctor who treats bone injuries or diseases.

Orthopedists often examine babies to see that their bones are developing well, but they are generally more involved with treating bone problems of adults.

PEDANTIC

Narrow-mindedly adhering to minor rules; stressing trivial points of learning.

The professor's lecture on the Middle Ages was pedantic and did not give the students a real grasp of what life was really like in those remote times.

PEDAGOGUE

A teacher, usually one who is dogmatic.

In the informal modern school there is less of a gap between teacher and pupil, and teachers are not regarded as pedagogues but as guides and facilitators.

PEL

Meaning: To push, to drive.

Origin: Latin, *pellere*, to thrust.

One of the first things you learn to say when you're beginning to study French is *Je m'appele* _____, meaning "My name is_____," or literally, "I put myself before you as _____." This sentence uses the French verb "appeler," *to name or call*, which comes from the Latin "appellare", *to thrust*. From this root, English derives the word APPEAL.

When you appeal to someone, you thrust yourself upon him for help or mercy; or to use the French derivation, you call upon him.

COMPULSIVE

Acting as though there were an inner drive; responding to an irresistible impulse to perform an irrational act.

Mrs. Brown is compulsive about cleanliness and cannot tolerate even a speck of dust.

REPULSIVE

Finding something so bad you want to push it away.

Joan found Tom's pimples repulsive.

REPEL

To cause dislike.

To their mutual surprise and chagrin, John was repelled by Mary's new perfume.

REPEL

To push back; to ward off.

When the burglar tried to enter the apartment through the window, the dog quickly repelled him.

EXPEL

To force out.

Jim took a deep breath and then expelled it, blowing out all the birthday candles at once.

EXPEL

To dismiss, to make leave.

John was expelled from school for smoking in the locker room.

PROPEL

To push forward.

With one big push, John propelled Jim across the ravine.

IMPEL

To push from within.

As soon as the dog spotted the cat, he was impelled to chase it.

IMPULSIVE

Acting without conscious thought; acting on sudden drives from within.

John is so impulsive he can never make plans in advance.

COMPULSORY

Forcing; required; obligatory.

In Israel, military service is compulsory for both women and men.

COMPULSION

Force; coercion.

He did not really want to attend the party, but was under family compulsion to go.

DISPEL

To drive away.

The good news dispelled the gloom that had enveloped everyone.

COMPELLING

Forcing attention.

The book was so compelling, I couldn't put it down until I had finished reading it.

Forceful.

The teacher felt that going to his sister's graduation was not a sufficiently compelling reason for Johnny to miss school.

COMPEL

To force or push together.

Johnny was compelled to take a violin lesson every Saturday afternoon.

IMPULSE

A sudden drive to act.

The girl's hair looked so soft and beautiful he had an impulse to stroke it.

PROPELLER

A blade that drives a ship or a plane forward.

Jet planes do not use propellers.

REPELLENT

Keeping out.

Mary wore her water repellent raincoat when she went out to spray the yard with insect repellent.

PULSE

The rhythmic beat as the blood is pushed through the arteries.

The doctor felt the pulse of the man who had been hit by the car, and was relieved to find it normal.

PEND

Meaning: To hang, to weigh, to pay out, to think.

Origin: Latin, *pendere*, to hang.

In the course of its interesting history, the Latin root "pend," which means *to hang,* accumulated a variety of associations, connotations, and additional meanings. Two of the first extensions of the root were the meanings: *to weigh* and *to pay.* These meanings were derived in the following way:

In very ancient days, there were no coins. Merchants paid for goods with bulk gold and silver which they had to weigh out on delicate hanging scales. So the root "pend" came to mean *to weigh* and, eventually, *to pay out money,* as in the words EXPENSE and RECOMPENSE.

Many of the words we use today to name various coins come from the word WEIGH. The English *pound,* the Spanish *peso,* and the Hebrew *shekel* all mean a bit of metal of a certain weight, hence, of a certain value.

It is not hard to see how the act of weighing came to mean *judging:* a quantity was *weighed* and its worth *judged.* Ultimately, the meaning was extended as the word was applied to abstract ideas in addition to tangible objects. Thus, when we WEIGH a matter we *judge* its importance. And from the idea of judging came the general idea of thinking. The word PONDER originally meant to weigh, but it now usually means *to think.*

SPEND

To use up; to pay out; to pass.

On their vacation, they spent most of their time and money shopping in Paris.

PONDER

To think deeply, to meditate.

He pondered over the puzzle for a long time until he solved it.

SUSPENDERS

A pair of straps worn over the shoulders from which the trousers hang.

John prefers to wear suspenders rather than a belt to hold his pants up.

DISPENSARY

A place where medicine and medical treatment are given at small fees.

The mother took her child to the dispensary to get something for his cough.

SUSPENSE

Uncertainty.

We were in great suspense until the results of the medical examination came back.

RECOMPENSE

To repay, to reward.

The government recompensed the landlord for taking over his property.

STIPEND

Regular payment of a pension or an allowance.

The old man's only income was the small stipend he received from his son.

COMPENDIUM

A concise but comprehensive summary.

Her photograph album was a compendium of all the important events in her life.

WORDS COME IN FAMILIES 203

COMPENSATE

To pay.

Mary compensated the children for their work in washing the car and mowing the lawn.

To make up for.

John feels that the flexibility of his hours compensates for his low salary.

DEPEND

To hang on, to be controlled or influenced by something else.

Children depend on their parents to provide them with food.

To rely on for support or help.

Mary depended on her brother to drive her to work every day.

PENDULUM

A weight hung from a fixed point so that it moves freely back and forth.

The grandfather clock ticked loudly as the pendulum swung to and fro.

PERPENDICULAR

At right angles; vertical in relation to a horizontal plane.

To measure his son's height, he drew a line on the wall perpendicular to the floor.

PENSIVE

Deep in thought.

After she read the letter from her boyfriend in the Army, she sat quietly for a long time, looking very pensive.

PENDULOUS

Swinging freely.

Mary likes to wear pendulous earrings.

PONDEROUS

Very heavy, massive.

The elephant is a ponderous animal.

EXPEND

To pay out; to use up.

Mary expends a lot of energy running up and down the stairs.

DISPENSATION

A special exemption.

The Catholic couple asked the Pope for a dispensation so they could be divorced.

EXPENSIVE

High priced, costly.

Mrs. Smith wanted a new fur jacket, but her husband thought it was too expensive.

IMPENDING

Hanging in air, about to happen.

She was very busy making arrangements for the impending wedding.

DISPENSE

To give out.

The United States government dispenses 385 billion dollars a year.

To do without.

To finish on time, they dispensed with the speeches and got right to work.

POISE

Balance; ease of manner.

Everyone envies Mary for her poise in meeting new people.

Filled with indecision.

John stood on the street corner, poised between choosing to take a bus or a taxi.

INDEPENDENT

Free from the influence or control of others, self-reliant.

John is an independent thinker and is not easily swayed by the opinions of others.

COMPENSATION

Suitable payment for a loss or damage.

The Workmen's Compensation Act provides that workers be paid during their times of illness or injury.

EXPENSE

Money paid out, cost.

Living expenses today are so high that many people have trouble making ends meet.

Sacrifice.

By working day and night he managed to complete his project, but it was at the expense of his health.

PET

Meaning: To seek, to request, require.

Origin: Latin, *petere*, to seek.

People often engage in philosophical and moral discussions about whether COMPETITION is good or bad. One cannot deny that competition can be destructive. When competition is the chief motivation for achievement, it does not bring out the best human qualities. Cooperation is much more to be desired.

And yet, there is little doubt that when competition exists, standards are raised. For example, competition in sports often makes man reach for the best effort of which he is capable.

It is interesting to note that the word COMPETENT is directly related to COMPETITION, and literally means *being able to compete*.

IMPETUOUS

Acting suddenly, impulsive.

When the baby saw the dog, he made an impetuous move to grab its tail.

COMPETE

To be in rivalry, to enter a contest.

The children competed for prizes for the best Halloween costume.

COMPETENT

Capable, well qualified.

Mary is a very competent swimmer and works as a lifeguard at a summer camp.

APPETITE

A desire, especially for food.

The pleasant smells coming from the kitchen stimulated his appetite.

IMPETUS

A driving force.

He ran across the grass with his kite until it had enough impetus to soar through the air.

Motive.

After Mary broke up with her boyfriend, she had very little impetus to go to parties.

PETULANT

Impatient, peevish, bad-tempered.

Although he was very tired, the petulant youngster refused to go to sleep.

PERPETUAL

Lasting forever.

After World War I, an unknown French soldier was buried under the Arch of Triumph in Paris and a perpetual flame burns in his honor.

Constant.

She is a pleasant person and has a perpetual smile on her face.

PETITION

A formally drawn-up request, usually to someone in authority.

The students were furious when their favorite teacher was fired, and they drew up a petition requesting that the principal rehire him.

REPETITIOUS

Saying or doing something over and over.

The speeches were repetitious and made the meeting very boring.

REPEAT

To say or do again.

John tries very hard never to repeat a mistake.

PHIL

Meaning: To love.

Origin: Greek, *philos*, loving, tending toward.

Love, as everyone knows, makes the world go round. And, as everyone knows, there are different kinds of love. Physical or sexual love is related to the Latin root "amor." Spiritual or intellectual love is expressed in the root "phil."

If you know anyone named PHILLIP, ask him if he is fond of horses. The name Philip combines "philos" which means *love* with "hippos" which means *a horse*.

The Greek statesman Demosthenes achieved fame as a great political orator. In 351 B.C., he delivered the first of three impassioned speeches warning the Greeks against Philip II of Macedon. From this event came the word PHILIPPIC, which means *a bitter verbal attack against someone or something*.

PHILANTHROPIST

A person who gives generously to charitable causes, a lover of mankind.

Many wealthy industrialists, such as Henry Ford and John D. Rockefeller, were philanthropists who donated millions to improve the health and welfare of people.

BIBLIOPHILE

A person who loves books.

Mr. Jones is a bibliophile and has a wonderful collection of rare, leather-bound books.

PHILHARMONIC

A symphonic orchestra, a society that sponsors an orchestra.

Mary had a subscription to the Boston Philharmonic concert series.

PHILOLOGY

Linguistics, the study of language.

John was fascinated with the origin and history of words and wanted to study philology.

PHILOSOPHY

The study of the principles of knowledge.

René Descartes is considered to be the founder of modern philosophy.

A person's system of perspective, outlook.

John's philosophy of life is to enjoy the moment rather than plan for the future.

The general principles underlying any subject.

The school program is based on Dewey's philosophy of education: that children learn by doing, not by being told.

PHILANDERER

A man who carries on many love affairs.

Mary did not take John's professions of love seriously because she knew he was a philanderer.

PHILATELIST

A stamp collector.

President Roosevelt was a philatelist and had a valuable collection.

HEMOPHILIA

Hereditary disease in which blood does not clot quickly enough and excessive bleeding results from cuts.

He used an electric shaver rather than a razor; he had to be very careful to avoid cuts since he had hemophilia.

PHILTER

A magic potion to make a person fall in love.

In Shakespeare's A Midsummer Night's Dream, *the mischievous Puck gives a love philter to the wrong person.*

PHOBIA

Meaning: A strong fear, an aversion based on fear.

Origin: Greek, *phobos*, fear.

The range of man's fears is extensive. Some of these fears are sensible, serving to protect man from wandering unwittingly into danger. Other fears seem baseless. Everything and anything may be the subject of fear—open spaces or closed spaces, other men, snakes, cats, dogs, to name a few.

There are actually about 200 words which combine with the root "phobia" to describe man's different fears. Below is a selection of just a few of man's phobias.

PHOBIA

Irrational or excessive fear of some particular thing.

John is a perfectionist and has a phobia about making mistakes.

ACROPHOBIA

Fear of high places.

People who have acrophobia will not be found mountain climbing.

HYDROPHOBIA

Rabies; disease caused by being bitten by an infected dog, characterized by inability to swallow water.

All dogs must get shots to prevent them from getting hydrophobia.

XENOPHOBIA

A morbid dislike or hatred of strangers or foreigners.

Many people who are prejudiced against minority groups actually suffer from the disease of xenophobia.

CLAUSTROPHOBIA

Fear of enclosed, tight, narrow places.

The woman suffered from claustrophobia and refused to enter the apartment house elevator.

AGORAPHOBIA

Fear of open or public places.

The man who suffered from agoraphobia shut himself in his room and wouldn't come out.

ALEUROPHOBIA

Fear of cats.

My aunt will not visit me because I have a cat and she has aleurophobia.

HELIOPHOBIA

A morbid fear of the sun.

A person suffering from heliophobia prefers to work at night.

PHON

Meaning: Sound.

Origin: Greek, *phone*, sound, voice.

There was a time when the spoken word, no matter how beautiful, eloquent, or important, could not be preserved. The voices of singers, actors, orators lingered on only in the memories of those who had heard them. What would we not give to hear the actual voice of Shakespeare acting in one of his plays, or of Lincoln delivering the Gettysburg Address.

And then, in 1878, Thomas A. Edison built the first successful PHONOGRAPH, which recorded sound on wax cylinders. As tinny, raucous, and uncertain as the first instruments were, they did preserve for posterity the spoken or sung words of the day. Of course, today we reproduce sound with startling fidelity through new improved techniques and instruments.

SYMPHONY

A pleasant harmony of sounds produced by many instruments playing together.

Beethoven never heard his own magnificent Ninth Symphony because by the time he completed it he was almost completely deaf.

TELEPHONE

Instrument for conveying speech over distances.

The first words spoken over the telephone: "Mr. Watson, come here, I want you," were uttered by its inventor, Alexander Graham Bell, in 1876.

EUPHONY

Sound with a pleasing quality.

Even cat-lovers must agree that cats wailing in the alleys at night do not produce euphony.

MICROPHONE

A small instrument for intensifying sound.

There was something wrong with the microphone and the audience could not hear the speaker.

CACOPHONY

Harsh, jarring sound, discord.

Today many modern musicians deliberately introduce cacophony into their compositions.

EUPHEMISM

A milder word or phrase substituted for a harsher one.

Many people use the euphemism "pass away" because they find the word die *too unpleasant.*

PHONETICS

The study of the sounds of language.

Many children are taught phonetics when they are learning to read so that they may sound out the written words.

PLIC PLY

Meaning: To fold, to bend.

Origin: Latin, *plicare*, to fold.
French, *plier*, to bend.

It is fitting that the root "ply," meaning *to bend,* has developed an utterly astounding number of adapted meanings.

The advantages of being SUPPLE are clearly observable. In fact, we were all, so to speak, weaned on the notion. We all remember the childhood lullaby, "Rockabye Baby, on the tree top." From this soothing song, we absorbed an incontestable bit of folk wisdom: The bough that does not bend, breaks.

From quite a different source, we learn how hard it is to veer off a course once we are bent in that direction. Alexander Pope, in his *Moral Essays,* cautions about those all-important early years: "Just as the twig is bent, the tree's inclin'd."

COMPLICATED

Intricate, involved, hard to understand or untangle.

The directions he gave us for getting to his house were so complicated that we could not follow them and got completely lost.

IMPLICATE

To involve, to intertwine.

Kissinger was not implicated in the Watergate Affair.

PLY

To work.

Mary's uncle is a carpenter and plies his trade diligently.

To bombard.

The students plied the actor with questions about Hollywood.

To travel back and forth.

The pilot plies his way between Europe and America.

APPLY

To put on.

She applied cream to his badly sunburned skin.

APPLY

To use.

When the door would not open, he applied pressure to make it open.

APPLY

To fit.

The parking regulations do not apply on Sunday.

APPLY

To concentrate on.

After his vacation, he applied himself seriously to his work.

APPLY

To make a request.

Mary applied for a job at a camp for the summer.

PLIERS

A tool for bending or cutting wire.

He used pliers to fix the lamp.

SIMPLE

Easy to do or understand.

John found the math test very simple.

Having few parts, uncomplicated.

They bought the child a simple puzzle.

Plain, unadorned.

Mary wore a simple but elegant dress to the wedding.

DUPLICATE

To fold in two or make double, to repeat exactly.

The ballet dancer could not duplicate the fantastic leap he had made at the earlier performance.

An exact copy.

He made out the contract in duplicate, keeping one copy for his files, and mailing the other copy to the company.

IMPLY

To indicate indirectly.

Although he didn't say anything, he implied that he agreed.

To include as a necessary part.

Running a democratic classroom implies that the students have some freedom of choice.

SUPPLE

Flexible, easily bent.

Mary is a good athlete because she has a supple body.

REPLY

To answer, to respond.

I have to reply to the wedding invitation I received.

PLYWOOD

Thin layers of wood folded or pressed together.

John bought some plywood to make a bookcase.

SUPPLICATION

A humble request, prayer or petition.

The king listened to his subject's supplication for mercy and granted it.

PERPLEX

To intertwine and make confusing; to puzzle.

The police were completely perplexed about how the robbers had managed to break into the vault without setting off the alarm.

COMPLEX

Made up of many interwoven parts, complicated, not simple.

The teacher's explanation of the theory of atomic energy was so complex, half the class could not understand it.

PLIANT, PLIABLE

Easily bent, easily influenced, adaptable.

The child is very pliant and does exactly what his parents tell him.

EXPLICIT

Leaving nothing implied, clearly stated.

It is easy to know where you stand with John because he makes his feelings explicit.

MULTIPLY

To cause to increase.

When he lost his self-confidence, his errors began to multiply.

REPLICA

A copy or reproduction, facsimile.

The museum sells replicas of famous pieces of sculpture.

PON   POSE

Meaning: To put, to place, to set.

Origin: Latin, *ponere*, to place.

You may be surprised to learn that the term POST OFFICE comes from the Latin root "pon." In French, the Latin "ponere" became *poser*, and the root came into English in both forms.

In olden days, mail was delivered quite differently from the way it is delivered today. Throughout the country, there existed a series of stations. At each of these stations, relays of fresh men and fresh horses were posted to carry letters and packages from one stage of the route to the next. Thus the POST OFFICE was a stage or station of the post route, and a POSTMAN was a man placed along the route to deliver mail.

COMPOSITE

Made up of various parts.

The new building was a strange composite of different styles of architecture.

DISPOSABLE

Easy to get rid of.

Disposable diapers are a big help to mothers of young children.

POSE

To sit as a model.

The artist needed a model to pose for his painting.

An attitude assumed before people.

Mary always looks very calm, but it's really a pose to cover up her nervousness.

To put forward.

When the baby sitter didn't show up, it posed a big problem for the parents.

POSTER

A large printed sheet to advertise or publicize something.

The travel posters were so beautiful, Mary put them up on her wall as decorations.

COMPONENT

A part, ingredient.

He could not finish putting his hi-fi set together because he was missing one of the components.

OPPOSE

To put something in front of, to block.

John applied to the local university because his parents were opposed to his leaving home.

PROPONENT

A person who supports a cause.

Secretary Kissinger is a proponent of détente as a means of avoiding nuclear war.

POSTPONE

To put off until later, delay.

The meeting had to be postponed because of the chairman's illness.

COMPOSE

To put together.

Salt is composed of one part sodium and one part chloride.

To create.

Beethoven composed some of the greatest music ever written.

To calm down.

Before going on stage, she composed herself by breathing deeply.

COMPOUND

A mixture, something composed by mixing two or more parts.

The druggist followed the doctor's prescription in making the medicinal compound.

PROPOSAL

A plan.

John's proposal was that we spend our summer vacation camping in the national parks out West.

An offer of marriage.

Mary was amused by Jim's proposal of marriage.

DEPOSIT

To put money in a bank.

John deposited his savings in the bank.

To leave in place.

When the Nile River rises it deposits a layer of mud on the land.

To set down.

The sit-in strikers deposited themselves in the principal's office and refused to leave.

DEPOSE

To put down from office, to remove.

Juan and Eva Peron were each deposed from the office of President of Argentina by military coups.

PREPOSITION

A relation word (usually placed before a noun or pronoun) that connects one part of the sentence to another.

Writers once tried to avoid ending a sentence with a preposition, as in: "What would you use that for?"

DISPOSAL

Putting away, getting rid of.

A modern method of garbage disposal is incineration.

Settling of affairs, arrangement.

The children met to arrange for the disposal of their deceased father's property.

Availability.

The chairman of the department is always at the disposal of the teachers.

EXPOSITION

Explanation in detail, to clarify, to set forth.

The preacher's exposition on the evils of drink made the congregation restless.

A public display of new artistic and industrial products.

We went to see the latest electronic equipment on display at the exposition.

DISPOSED

Inclined, having a certain tendency.

Mary's English teacher is favorably disposed toward Mary and overlooks her shortcomings.

EXPONENT

A person who explains or interprets a certain idea.

John Dewey was one of the foremost exponents of progressive education.

EXPOSE

To lay open, to disclose, to exhibit.

When all the details of the Watergate Affair were exposed, Americans were deeply shocked.

To deprive of shelter.

The windows of their house were broken and the family was exposed to wind, rain, and cold.

PROPOSE

To place an offer before somebody.

When John proposed to Mary, she told him that she loved him but did not want to get married just yet.

To intend.

Jim proposes to go to law school after he graduates from college.

To put forth.

One of the guests proposed a toast to the hostess of the dinner party.

To nominate.

Mary was proposed for president of the Student Council.

POSITIVE

Definitely set, admitting no question or change, sure.

The woman thought she could identify the man who had robbed her, but she was not absolutely positive.

Adding something helpful, constructive.

The teacher's criticism of the student's work included some positive suggestions.

IMPOSE

To place a burden upon.

The government has imposed high taxes on cigarettes and alcohol.

To force oneself on others.

Mary doesn't like to impose on her mother to baby sit for her.

DISPOSITION

Nature, temperament, habitual ways of acting.

Mary has a very sweet disposition and never says an unkind word about anyone.

OPPOSITE

Extremely different, contrary.

It is very difficult for Mr. and Mrs. Smith to go shopping together because their tastes are completely opposite.

OPPOSITE

End to end or face to face.

The couple sat opposite each other.

OPPONENT

A person who is against you in a fight, game, contest, argument.

At the end of the tennis match, the opponents shook hands.

POST

A place where a soldier or policeman is stationed.

The soldier was punished severely for falling asleep at his post.

Mail.

The wedding invitation came in this morning's post.

To put up a notice.

The students' final grades were posted on the bulletin board.

PROPOSITION

A business proposal

The employer made the workers a proposition for a profit-sharing plan.

A statement that is to be proved true; assumption.

A democracy is based on the proposition that all men have equal rights.

SUPPOSE

To think, imagine, presume.

I suppose the children will help with the moving.

To be expected.

The babysitter is supposed to come at seven o'clock.

POSITION

Where someone or something is.

The teacher placed himself in a position so that he could see all his students at once.

A person's attitude or opinion.

The senator's position on freezing wages was not popular with the labor unions.

A job.

Mr. Smith holds a very important position in his firm and is responsible for major policy decisions.

PORT

Meaning: To carry.

Origin: Latin, *portare*, carry.

To TRANSPORT, or *carry* things from one place to another is crucial to man's existence. The world would be very different, indeed, if materials that grew or were produced in one place could not be brought to other areas. Of what use would a million rubber trees be in Asia, or a hundred million cotton plants in India?

The need to transport things was recognized a very long time ago, when the only means to do so was by carrying them. The two earliest mechanical means of transportation were the wheel and the boat. We do not know exactly when or how they were developed, because they predate recorded history.

In 1769, James Watt perfected his steam engine. This invention, which had the capacity to turn the wheels of vast, complicated machinery, was influential in bringing about the Industrial Revolution. It was not long before the steam engine was applied to means of transportation.

By placing the steam engine on a boat, Robert Fulton invented the steamboat. With this invention, a boat could move under its own power; boats, and the men who steered them, were no longer at the mercy of uncertain winds.

In 1815, George Stephenson created a small locomotive by mounting the steam engine on a wagon. No longer would man have to rely upon the slow pulling of wagons by horses. He now had the means to transport goods quickly and easily.

In 1903, the most dramatic change in transportation took place. At Kitty Hawk, North Carolina, Wilbur and Orville Wright attached an engine they had designed to a glider, and made the first successful flight in a power-driven airplane. Having conquered the land and the sea, man was now in command of the air as well.

IMPORTUNE

To beg or urge repeatedly, literally, without a harbor.

The woman importuned the doctor to help her baby.

PORTER

A person who carries luggage.

The porter took their luggage from the terminal and put it in their car.

SUPPORT

To carry the weight of; to give help or conduct to.

The old woman leaned on the young man for support as she crossed the street.

To provide with money.

When prices rose, he found it hard to support his wife and children on his small salary.

To be in favor of.

Not enough people supported the Equal Rights Amendment to get it accepted in New York.

COMPORTMENT
DEPORTMENT

Behavior, conduct.

The child was aware that the occasion was a solemn one and his comportment was excellent.

IMPORTANT

Carrying significance, value, or power.

It was very important for Mary to be on time because she had an important job to perform.

SPORT

Recreation, pastime, amusement (this word is a contracted form of disport).

John swims for sport.

Organized game or activity.

Archery goes back 20,000 years and may be the world's oldest sport.

A person with a good ability to take defeat.

Mary hated to lose the contest, but she was a good sport about it.

A showy person.

Jim leaves huge tips in restaurants to show what a sport he is.

EXPORT

To carry out, to send from one country to another.

The United States exports vast quantities of machinery and food stuffs all over the world.

PORT

Where the ship docks and the goods are carried in and out of the city, harbor.

Rotterdam is the great port city of Holland.

OPPORTUNITY

An appropriate or favorable time or occasion.

After failing the test the first time, John asked his teacher for another opportunity to show what he could do.

Good chance.

Mary is a ballet buff and never misses an opportunity to attend a performance.

OPPORTUNE

Well timed.

He was offered the job at the most opportune time, just when he was about to use up all his savings.

IMPORT

To carry in, to bring into one country from another.

The United States imports vast quantities of coffee from Brazil.

REPORT

To give an account of.

A good journalist will report the facts without editorializing.

DISPORT

To carry oneself away from one's daily cares and worries, to indulge in amusement.

Many a busy executive disports himself on the golf course.

DEPORT

To carry away, to expel from a country.

When people enter a country illegally, without passports or visas, they are in danger of being deported if found out.

TRANSPORTATION

Means of getting from one place to another.

John does not own a car and relies on public transportation.

PRIM PRIN PRESS

Meaning: To press, to squeeze.

Origin: Latin, *premere*, to press.

From its earliest primitive beginning in ancient Babylonia, PRINTING was a form of pressure. The Babylonians used seals and stamps to press imprints in clay.

Before the development of printing from type, all books were laboriously written by hand. Monks throughout Europe kept alive the art of writing books, often with exquisite color and beauty. It could take as much as six months to copy books in this way. To this day, the Torah, the magnificent scroll of the Old Testament that is kept in the ark of every synagogue, is hand inscribed.

In ancient times, books were written on parchment—the prepared skins of animals—and could last for centuries. Books were enormously valuable; one volume could cost as much as a hundred pieces of gold. The Bible in a church was chained to the pulpit.

To own a book was a sign of wealth. To read a book was a sign of rare intellectual distinction. There was, perhaps, only one individual in an entire village who could read.

Although printing probably originated in China, the printing of the first European book from movable type is generally attributed to Johann Gutenberg. In Mainz, Germany, around 1456, Gutenberg printed the Mazarin Bible on a press he had built.

At this time, printing was still clumsy and costly. The term used to describe books printed before 1500 is INCUNABULA, meaning *the cradle or infant stage*.

With the coming of the Industrial Revolution, printing machinery was run by steam, and later by oil and electricity. Gutenberg's first hand press was like a little toy compared to today's giant power presses. In recent years, the development of electronic devices has revolutionized the printing industry. Today, type can be set by photographic means.

COMPRESS

To press together; a pad of folded cloth.

The nurse applied a cold compress to the forehead of the feverish patient.

To make compact.

A good poet can compress many beautiful thoughts and feelings into a few well-chosen words.

IMPRINT

Mark by pressing or stamping.

Before the cement had a chance to dry, many footsteps were imprinted on the sidewalk.

Implanted in the memory.

The horror movie left an unforgettable imprint on the child's mind.

FINGERPRINT

The lines on the tip of the finger.

The police can identify people by their fingerprints because no two are exactly alike.

IMPRESSIONISM

A style of art that developed in France in the late 19th century.

Manet, Monet, Renoir, and Degas advocated impressionism.

IMPRESSION

The way things appear to you; a mark or imprint left by something.

Lincoln's Gettysburg Address, with its affirmation of the democratic ideal, made a powerful impression on the American people.

DEPRESSION

Extreme sadness.

The death of her child threw her into a deep depression.

A period in which economic conditions are very poor.

During the depression of the 1930's, unemployment was widespread.

SUPPRESS

To put down, to crush.

The government sent the militia out to suppress the revolt.

To conceal, to hold back, to check.

Mary didn't want to offend her guest and tried to suppress her yawn.

OPPRESS

To press down hard upon the mind and spirit; to burden, to tyrannize.

The dictator who tried to oppress his people was eventually overthrown.

EXPRESS

To picture, show.

She expressed her appreciation with a kiss.

Exact or special.

We went to the museum with the express purpose of looking at Picasso's "Guernica."

High speed.

It was an express train and made very few stops.

REPRESS

To hold back.

He repressed his emotions in order not to break down at the funeral.

To keep things in the unconscious.

We all try to repress the memories of unhappy events, especially those from early childhood.

IMPRIMATUR

Let it be printed; approval, sanction.

The article on Joan of Arc was published under the imprimatur of the Catholic Church.

REPRIMAND

To scold.

The teacher reprimanded the student for being late.

IMPRESSIONABLE

Sensitive, easily influenced.

Mary is worried about the impact of television on her impressionable younger brother.

DEPRESS

To press down, to lower in spirits; to discourage.

Newspaper accounts of murder, violence, and disasters can depress any reader.

PRESSURE

Compelling influence.

John's friends put pressure on him to make him change his mind and join them at the party.

Strain.

Mary is under much pressure to get high grades so she can get into college.

Weight or force brought to bear.

Mr. Smith is on a salt-free diet because he suffers from high blood pressure.

FOOTPRINT

Mark left by a foot.

The children compared the sizes of their footprints in the snow.

PUNCT PUNG PUG

Meaning: To strike or to prick.

Origin: Latin, *pungere*, to prick, to puncture.
Latin, *punctus*, a point.

This root has developed a bewildering family of words which, on the surface, do not seem to be related. Yet if we scratch beneath the surface, we can discern the derivation from the root which means *to strike,* or *to prick.* With some of the words in this family, the literal meaning has become figurative, and is thus less easy to trace back to the root.

In the word PUGILIST, meaning a *fighter,* the root is obvious—a fighter is someone who *strikes* his opponent. And when you are filled with COMPUNCTION, you are conscience-*stricken.*

The root meaning is less literal, but still discernible in such words as PUNCTUATE *(to mark the points and dots sharply)* and APPOINTMENT *(a point in time fixed by mutual agreement).*

IMPINGE

To strike; to break in, to intrude.

He tried to sleep but the sounds of the traffic impinged upon his ears.

IMPINGE

To violate, to interfere.

Mary felt that her mother-in-law was impinging on her right to raise her children in her own way.

COMPUNCTION

Remorse, regret for wrong doing, a sharp feeling of guilt, a twinge of conscience.

He was filled with compunction for having lied to his mother.

PUNCTUATE

To use certain standardized marks such as commas, colons, periods, in a written sentence.

Sometimes the way you punctuate a sentence can make a big difference in meaning, as in:
Secretary quits, criticizing boss.
Secretary quits criticizing boss.

PUGNACIOUS

Disposed to fight, quarrelsome.

John tries to make up for his small size by his pugnacious manner.

REPUGNANT

Distasteful.

Coarse four letter words are still repugnant to many people.

APPOINTMENT

Arrangement to meet at a set place and time.

She was in a great rush because she didn't want to be late for her dentist's appointment.

DISAPPOINT

To break a promise.

Mary said she would come to help me with my work, but she disappointed me and didn't show up.

To fail to satisfy the hopes or expectations.

John was very disappointed when he didn't get into medical school.

IMPACT

Impression.

The doctor's report made a big impact on him and he resolved to stop smoking.

Collision.

His car hit the tree with a terrific impact and he was killed instantly.

POINT

A sharp end.

My pencil point keeps breaking.

A particular time.

Mary has just started high school and at this point she doesn't know whether she will go to college.

The main idea or purpose.

John couldn't see the point of taking his bathing suit since it was too cold to go swimming.

Unit of scoring.

Jim was responsible for making most of the points scored by his basketball team.

To show with a finger.

The guide pointed out all the historic landmarks.

PUNCTURE

A prick or a perforation.

A small piece of glass punctured his bicycle tire.

PUGILIST

A boxer, prize fighter.

One of the most talented and colorful pugilists is the heavyweight champion, Muhammad Ali.

PUNGENT

Sharp in taste or smell.

The cheese was aged until it was very pungent.

Piercing, penetrating.

I enjoyed reading the review of the new play because the critic's remarks were pungent.

EXPUNGE

To strike or blot out, erase, delete.

No matter how hard she tried to forget him, she could not expunge the memory of her exboyfriend.

PUNCTUAL

Prompt, coming exactly at the appointed time.

He was punctual in paying his rent, sending the landlord a check on the first of every month.

APPOINT

To select for an office or position.

John was very proud to be appointed captain of the soccer team.

POIGNANT

Sharply distressing.

We were very moved by the poignant story of the children orphaned in the war.

Q U E R   Q U E S

Meaning: To ask, to seek.

Origin: Latin, *quaerere*, to ask, to inquire.

Words often have shades of meaning that reverberate profound philosophical distinctions. Sometimes, just by juxtaposing words that are listed far apart in the dictionary, we gain added insights into their meaning.

For example, the two words REQUEST, *to ask,* and QUEST, *to seek*, are similar in linguistic form, but they nevertheless signal an important difference: A person on a quest is searching out something for himself; a person who makes a request is asking for something from someone else.

An interesting distinction exists, too, between the words INQUISITIVE and ACQUISITIVE. An inquisitive person is likely to accumulate information or knowledge, while an acquisitive person is busy amassing material objects.

ACQUIRE

To get possession of.

He kept practicing his golf stroke until he acquired great skill.

To gain or obtain.

Men strive to acquire enough money to provide comfortably for themselves and their families.

CONQUER

To win, especially by fighting.

Belligerent nations try to conquer new territory through war.

To get possession or control of.

Mary worked very hard to conquer her fear of the deep water.

INQUISITION

An official investigation.

In the 13th century, the Roman Catholic Church set up a court to conduct an inquisition into heresy and to punish persons who did not adhere to the tenets of the Church.

QUEST

A seeking, pursuit; a journey in search of some particular thing.

A famous Canadian physician and teacher, Sir William Osler, said, "The quest for righteousness is Oriental, the quest for knowledge, Occidental."

PREREQUISITE

Required beforehand.

A prerequisite condition to being President of the United States is that you be a native-born citizen over the age of 35.

INQUIRE

To seek information, to ask questions about.

When we met again after many years, we first inquired after the health of our families.

QUESTIONNAIRE

A printed form used to gather information.

When he applied for the job, he was asked to fill out a questionnaire about his qualifications and experience.

REQUEST

The act of asking.

The teacher granted the student's request to change his seat.

To ask politely.

The audience was requested not to smoke in the auditorium.

QUERY

A question, a doubt, to ask about.

There were many queries about the accuracy of the details in the new book about Kennedy.

REQUISITION

A formal written order for equipment or materials.

The captain put in a requisition to the Supply Corps for new uniforms for his men.

QUESTION

Something that is asked.

At the end of his lecture, the professor answered questions from the audience.

QUESTION

A doubt or uncertainty.

There is some question about whether the painting is an original.

QUESTION

To interrogate, to examine orally.

The lawyer questioned the witness about every detail.

REQUIRE

To have need of, to find necessary.

The plant required lots of light but very little water.

To demand authoritatively.

The men were required to wear jackets and ties for the wedding ceremony.

INQUEST

A coroner's investigation of a death.

An inquest is held in every case of murder.

INQUISITIVE

Curious, asking many questions.

The students were very inquisitive about the foreign visitor.

REG

Meaning: Straight, direct, to lead.

Origin: Latin, *regere*, to set straight, to guide, to rule.

The word root "reg" demonstrates once again how Latin words were absorbed into English in two ways, with related but different meanings. Sometimes, English adopted the French version of a Latin word, and sometimes the word entered the English language directly from the Latin.

Frequently, the hard "g" of Latin words was dropped in French, so that, for example, the Latin word for REGAL became ROYAL. The Latin word "regula" dropped its hard "g" and became the common English word RULER.

The word RULER neatly shows the dual meaning of the root "reg." One meaning is *a measuring rod,* usually a straight-edged strip of wood, metal, or plastic which is used to measure length or to draw a straight line. A second meaning of RULER is *a sovereign,* or *a person who governs*. Presumably, of course, a RULER is one who sets his subjects straight.

IRREGULAR

Uneven.

The mother cut the child's hair herself and left all the ends irregular.

Not according to the rule.

The student was asked to explain the reason for his irregular attendance.

CORRECT

To set right.

The teacher corrected the errors in the student's homework.

In accordance with the truth, accurate, free from errors.

Do you have the correct time?

DIRECTION

The line in which a moving person or thing goes.

We drove in a northeasterly direction for several miles.

Instruction for doing something or going somewhere.

Mary followed the directions on the box very carefully and the biscuits turned out beautifully.

An order or command.

The woman left directions for the maid to dust the furniture and vacuum the rugs.

REGIME

A system of rule or government.

The old regime in France fell with the revolution of 1789.

DIRECTOR

A person who conducts or manages a group.

The actors were confused because the director and the playwright disagreed in their interpretation of the play.

DIRECT

Straight, not roundabout.

We took the most direct route and got home very quickly.

Frank and straightforward.

The reporters were very pleased with the president's direct and open answers to all their questions.

To manage or guide.

The sales manager directed the salesman to be courteous and helpful.

REIGN

The period of rule of the king.

It was during the reign of Queen Victoria in England that the ethic of duty and strict morality took hold.

UPRIGHT

Straight up, erect, in a vertical position.

The strong wind blew everything over and not a chair was left upright.

Honest, just.

The storekeeper was well liked because he treated his customers in an upright manner.

REGIMENT

A military unit.

The colonel ordered the regiment to prepare for battle.

A large number.

A whole regiment of ants attacked the food that was left in the dog bowl.

To treat in a strict or uniform manner.

Wearing long hair and casual clothes was the students' way of rebelling against being regimented.

REGULAR

According to the rule; normal, habitual.

When his wife took ill, he found it difficult to follow his regular schedule.

REGENT

One who rules in place of a king.

The Regency style originated about 1811, when the Prince of Wales (later King George IV) was appointed regent because King George III's infirmities made him unfit to rule.

ERECT

Upright, vertical.

The children stood as erect as soldiers.

ERECT

To put up or build.

The farmer erected a shed for storing his wood.

RIGHT

Correct, good.

The father wondered whether he had done the right thing when he sent his son money.

Not left.

Soldiers always salute with their right hands.

Exactly or immediately.

The teacher shouted at the boy, "You put that scissors right here on my desk right now!"

A just claim.

In a democracy, all people have the right to choose who will represent them in government.

RECTIFY

To put straight, to correct.

The customer pointed out that there was an error in the bill and the manager rectified it.

DIRECTORY

A book listing names and addresses.

We looked in the telephone directory to find the nearest shoemaker.

RECTOR

A clergyman; head of a university.

The rector encouraged the members of his parish to be active in community affairs.

REGALIA

The insignia of royalty; the decorations or insignia of any office or order; finery.

The Shriners came in full regalia for their annual ball.

REGAL

Kingly or royal.

The children arranged a regal banquet for their parents' 50th wedding anniversary.

RIGHTEOUS

Doing what is right, virtuous.

He felt righteous when he returned the wallet he had found in the street to its owner.

REGULATION

A rule, law.

A careful driver obeys all the traffic regulations.

REGULATE

To control or direct.

The warden regulated every minute of the prisoners' lives.

To adjust.

My watch is running fast and I need to take it to the jeweler to be regulated.

R O G

Meaning: To seek, to ask.

Origin: Latin, *rogare*, to seek, to ask.

The root "rog," which means *to ask,* has also come to mean *to demand,* and *to demand unreasonably for oneself,* as in the word PREROGATIVE.

The word ARROGANT means *aggressively presumptuous.* An arrogant person is one who makes undue claims for himself.

Something very interesting once happened in France: a nation-wide poll was held among schoolchildren to find out who they believed was the greatest Frenchman.

People were sure that the children would choose Napoleon, the symbol of French national glory. But to everyone's surprise, the children chose the chemist Louis Pasteur. Evidently, the youngsters were put off by the ARROGANCE of Napoleon. Perhaps they regarded his ambitiousness as self-seeking, and thus believed Napoleon contributed little to the welfare of the nation. Pasteur, on the other hand, devoted his life to helping others; the children recognized this as true greatness.

ABROGATE

To repeal, to abolish, to annul by an authoritative act.

Congress once passed laws prohibiting the sale of liquor in the United States, but the 20th Amendment to the Constitution abrogated these laws, and now liquor may be sold.

PREROGATIVE

A privilege, an exclusive right attached to an office or a particular rank.

As president of the company, he had the prerogative of choosing his successor.

INTERROGATE

To question, to examine by asking questions.

For several hours, the police interrogated the man who was suspected of murder.

ARROGANT

Overbearing, full of a sense of self-importance.

The chairman was admired for his competence, but he was disliked for the arrogant way in which he ordered everyone about.

ARROGATE

To lay undue claim to, to claim proudly or con- temptuously.

Taking advantage of his fero- ciousness, the lion arrogated to himself most of the spoils.

DEROGATE

To disparage, to belittle, to seek to lower.

People who constantly dero- gate others are usually inse- cure about their own abilities.

RUPT

Meaning: To break.

Origin: Latin, *rumpere*, to break.

In the Middle Ages, when a merchant could no longer pay his debts, his creditors would break up the bench where he did his work, exchanged his money, or carried on his business. From this medieval practice came our word BANKRUPT.

The word BENCH came from the ancient form "banca."

ABRUPT

Broken away or off; unexpected, sudden.

The open-air concert came to an abrupt end when it started to rain.

DISRUPT

To break away, to break up.

The silence in the library was disrupted when someone dropped a book.

RUPTURE

A break, a breach.

A man with a ruptured appendix is very critically ill; unless promptly attended to, the infection may kill him.

ERUPT

To break out.

The volcano Vesuvius erupted in 79 A.D. and covered the entire city of Pompeii with volcanic ash.

BANKRUPT

Unable to pay one's debts.

The company operated at a loss for a year and was finally forced to declare itself bankrupt.

INTERRUPT

To break into, to stop temporarily.

The meeting was interrupted by an emergency announcement that the building had to be evacuated immediately.

ROUTINE

A regular or unvarying procedure.

The children took advantage of the fact that the substitute teacher was not familiar with the class routines and they were late for their activities.

CORRUPT

Unsound, rotten, as though altogether broken down and ruined.

A corrupt city administration looked the other way when public servants were freely taking bribes.

ROUTE

A road, a way, a course that you follow, the customary, well-beaten road.

Although we knew that the thruway was the shortest route, we decided to take the more scenic route.

S A L

Meaning: To leap.

Origin: Latin, *salire*, to leap.

An INSULT has come to mean *an act or a remark that hurts someone's feelings or diminishes his self-respect.* But originally, to insult someone literally meant *to leap upon him* or *to attack him.* The relationship between the original meaning of the word and its modern usage is expressed in the wise adage: "He who insults a person in public is like one who sheds blood."

In days past, a gentleman who had been insulted had no choice but to challenge the offender to a duel. Today, we try to handle insults maturely, and do not resort to violence.

Do you agree with Göethe that "No holiness requires us to submit to insult," or with Seneca that "It is often better not to see an insult than to avenge it"?

ASSAULT

An unlawful attack on a person, literally a leaping upon.

To everybody's horror, the lion assaulted the lion tamer in the middle of the circus act.

SOMERSAULT

A leap in which the person turns heels over head.

The children learned how to turn somersaults in their gym class.

RESULT

What leaps back, to happen as a consequence of something else.

The earthquake resulted in great loss of life and damage to property.

An effect or outcome.

As a result of his increased effort, his work improved greatly.

SALACIOUS

Lustful, like the male animal when he leaps on the female; obscene.

Sometimes there is a question about whether a publication is a work of literature or if it is merely salacious.

ASSAIL

To attack.

Many misfortunes assailed the poor man all at the same time—he lost his job, his wife fell ill, and his house was struck by lightning.

SALLY

A leaping forth; to go out.

As they finished their work, the students sallied forth from the building.

A sprightly remark.

John has a quick sense of humor and his jokes and sallies kept everyone at the party entertained.

DESULTORY

Disconnected and irregular, as though you were jumping or leaping around.

He made a desultory effort to improve his tennis, playing for three hours one day and then not playing again for two weeks.

RESILIENT

Leaping back, recovering quickly.

Young children are generally resilient and recover from accidents fairly quickly.

S C O P

Meaning: To look, to see.

Origin: Latin, *scopus*, view.

Greek, *skopos*, a spy, a watcher.

Overlooking Jerusalem there is a mountain from which one can see for miles and miles around. Its name—Mount Scopus—is quite appropriate, for the root "scop" means *to look* or *to see*.

The early Christians borrowed this word root to designate a religious or spiritual overseer, or BISHOP. Today, a bishop is a clergyman who oversees a diocese.

A bishop is also a chessman who oversees and therefore controls the diagonal row on which he is placed on the chessboard.

MICROSCOPE

An instrument that uses lenses to magnify objects invisible to the naked eye.

The biologist examined the tissue under the microscope.

STETHOSCOPE

An instrument used to examine the heart.

The doctor listened to the patient's heart through his stethoscope.

TELESCOPE

A tubelike instrument containing lenses and mirrors which makes distant objects appear nearer and larger.

The astronomer studied the stars through his telescope.

HOROSCOPE

A chart of the zodiacal signs or positions of the planets by which astrologers tell a person's character or future.

Many newspapers carry daily horoscopes which tell one's fortune by the date of one's birth.

SCOPE

Outlook; range of view.

The book was very broad in scope, covering the history of the theater from ancient Greece to modern times.

Extent of intellectual grasp.

The psychiatrist's lecture was beyond the scope of the average layman.

EPISCOPAL

Governed by bishops.

The Protestant Episcopal movement started in 1870 when the Vatican Council of the Roman Catholic Church rejected the idea that the authority to govern a church should rest in a body of bishops rather than in an individual.

KALEIDOSCOPE

A tube with bits of colored glass that reveals many symmetrical patterns when rotated; hence, anything that has constantly changing colors and patterns.

The sun shone through the window, creating a kaleidoscope of light and color on the floor.

PERISCOPE

A tubelike instrument using lenses and mirrors which enables one submerged in a submarine to see above the water.

The captain of the submarine spotted the oncoming war vessel through the periscope.

SCRIB SCRIPT

Meaning: To write.

Origin: Latin, *scribere*, to write.

The earliest writing consisted of pictures INSCRIBED on rock. We have found examples of picture writing in different parts of the world. The Lascaux cave paintings in France are believed to have been made over 15,000 years ago. Although such writings tell us something of our ancestors, we cannot interpret the language they used.

The system of picture writing was gradually refined; ultimately the Egyptian system of hieroglyphics was developed. This system remained in use until about 1000 B.C.

And then some unknown Semitic genius made a fantastic discovery: by using just twenty-two symbols he could represent all the sounds people made when they communicated with each other. He created twenty-two simple pictures which became the twenty-two letters of the original Phoenician alphabet. With this invention, it became possible for all the wisdom of man to be written down.

Animals teach their young the knowledge and skills that will enable them to survive on earth. But man is the only animal who can, in effect, transcend time. He can call upon the knowledge of those who have gone before him. Man can perform this magical feat of going beyond space and time, through written language.

INSCRIBE

To write in or on.

The names of the fallen soldiers were inscribed on a large stone monument.

SCRIBBLE

To write carelessly or illegibly.

The mother was dismayed to see that her child had scribbled all over the walls.

SCRIBE

A writer.

Before the days of printing, all books were laboriously handwritten by scribes.

MANUSCRIPT

A written or typewritten document.

The author sent his manuscript to the publisher and waited impatiently to find out whether it would be accepted for publication.

DESCRIBE

To tell or write about in words

He described his girlfriend to his mother in such glowing terms that his mother couldn't wait to meet her.

PROSCRIBE

To write before.

In ancient Rome, the names of those whose property or life was forfeit were proscribed, or published.

To forbid.

The Ten Commandments proscribe stealing and murder.

SUBSCRIBE

To sign your name at the bottom of a document; to agree to pay for a magazine for a specified period of time.

More people subscribe to the Reader's Digest *than to any other American magazine.*

To assent to, to believe in.

Some teachers subscribe to the idea that corporal punishment should be allowed in schools.

PRESCRIBE

To set down as a rule or direction; to write down medicine or treatment.

The doctor prescribed sunshine and exercise for the child who was recovering from the measles.

SCRIPT

A style of handwriting.

Hebrew and Arabic scripts go from right to left across the page.

The written part of a play.

The director read the script and decided to produce the play.

TRANSCRIBE

To make a copy of; to transliterate, or to replace the letters of one language by another.

The secretary was busy all afternoon transcribing and typing from her shorthand notes the letters her boss had dictated.

SCRIPTURES

The books of the Bible; the Bible.

The minister based his sermon on one of the verses from the Scriptures.

S E C

Meaning: To cut.

Origin: Latin, *secare*, to cut.

As part of their medical education, students must learn everything about the human body. To do so, they examine cadavers. Under the direction of their instructor, medical students DISSECT, or *cut up* dead bodies to observe the working of the human organism. Although this practice may seem fairly gruesome, it is necessary for the training of our future doctors.

Until recently, obtaining enough cadavers for dissection in medical schools was a problem. But lately, because of the high cost of a traditional funeral and burial, more people are ready to donate their bodies to science for the purpose of dissection and medical research.

SAW

A cutting tool, usually with sharp teeth; to cut.

Two men sawed down the huge tree.

INTERSECTION

A place where two roads meet or cut into each other.

There was a car accident at the intersection.

SCYTHE

A long-handled, long-bladed instrument for mowing.

For thousands of years before the reaper was invented, farmers cut their grain with scythes.

SEGMENT

A portion cut off, a division.

The mother divided the orange into segments so the children could share it.

SICKLE

A cutting tool with a crescent-shaped blade and a short handle.

The sickle, a very ancient agricultural cutting instrument, is a symbol on the Russian flag.

BISECT

To cut into two.

The road bisected the forest.

WORDS COME IN FAMILIES   263

SECTION

A piece cut out.

The hostess cut the pie into eight equal sections.

A part or division.

The reviewers criticized the section of the movie that depicted violence.

INSECT

A tiny animal that has six or more legs and no backbone, whose body is divided into three distinct parts.

Only one percent of all insects are harmful; the grasshopper and Japanese beetle destroy crops, for example, and the mosquito, tse-tse fly, and flea are disease carriers.

SECTOR

A district into which an area is divided.

After World War II, the city of Berlin was divided into two sectors: the eastern sector was placed under Soviet influence, and the western sector was put under the authority of the Allied powers.

S E D   S E S S

Meaning: To sit.

Origin: Latin, *sedere*, to sit.

An activity which requires one to sit rather than to move about is called SEDENTARY. Although in modern times there has been a great increase in mental stimulation, there has also been a decrease in movement. Practically all our amusements—watching television, attending ball games, going to the theater—are sedentary.

Ancient man exercised his body in the course of his daily activities—hunting animals, fleeing from danger, capturing women, and in a later period, working in the fields. He had no trouble falling asleep at night.

In modern times, our minds are overstimulated while our bodies get flabby. We spend our days in sedentary activities, and yet we find we need SEDATIVES to help us relax at night.

DISSIDENT

Sitting apart, differing in opinion.

At the political convention, efforts were made to meet the demands of dissident groups in order to present a united front.

SEDIMENT

Solid matter falling to the bottom of liquid.

People usually try to clear wine of sediment before drinking it.

SEAT

A place where a person sits, such as a chair, bench, or stool.

The auditorium had seats for 2,000 people.

PRESIDE, PRESIDENT

To sit in front of all others, to be in the position of authority.

The City Council is presided over by the mayor.

SETTLE

To put in order.

After the father died, the lawyer helped the family settle its affairs.

To stay in one place.

After moving around quite a bit, the family finally settled in Florida.

To reach an agreement.

The teacher quoted some facts to help settle the argument that broke out between the students.

SIT

To take a seat.

Please do not sit on the table.

To pose.

She went to the artist's studio to sit for her portrait.

To watch a baby.

Mary often sits for the young mother next door.

SUPERSEDE

To sit above, to take the place of.

The automobile superseded the horse and wagon in modern times.

INSIDIOUS

Sitting in wait, full of cunning, working secretly.

One student in the class was always critical of everything and had an insidious effect on class morale.

More dangerous than is apparent.

Although he had recovered from mononucleosis, the insidious disease left him with very little energy.

SESSION

Sitting together for a conference.

The judge called the court into session.

A school term.

The student made up his mind to work harder to improve his grades during the next session.

SEDATIVE

A drug that brings on calm or lessens pain.

He was in great pain after the operation and was given sedatives to help him sleep.

SET

To put in place.

Mary helped her mother set the table for the dinner party.

SET

A collection or group.

John has an unusual chess set that he got in India.

SET

Where something takes place.

The story was set in a small village in Europe.

To write down.

Right after his trip, he set down all his impressions in his diary.

To regulate.

He set the alarm to ring at eight o'clock.

To be fixed or rigid.

Once her mind is set, it is very difficult to make her change it.

To appoint a time.

We set a date for out next meeting.

SET

To arrange.

Mary had her hair washed and set in the beauty parlor.

RESIDE

To take up one's home, to live.

Over 8 million people reside in New York City.

S E N S   S E N T

Meaning: To feel, to think, to sense.

Origin: Latin, *sentire*, to feel, to perceive.

The word SENTENCE is crucial to two systems created by man —grammar and the law. The common denominator lies in the root "sent," *to think*.

In traditional grammar, a SENTENCE is defined as *a group of words expressing a complete thought*. A sentence reports what someone thinks or feels.

When a judge passes a SENTENCE, he announces the punishment for a convicted person. The sentence reflects the judge's opinion or sense of the case.

SCENT

A smell, an odor so distinctive that a person or an animal can be traced by it.

She tried various perfumes to see which scent she liked best.

SENSATION

Feeling, impression.

As he went higher and higher on the swing, the child had a sensation of flying.

SENSE

The power of feeling by touching, smelling, seeing, tasting and hearing.

He could sense that she was in the room even though he could not see her.

Intelligence, judgment.

You can trust John to use good sense in buying the present.

Meaning.

The poem made no sense to me.

DISSENT

To think differently, to disagree.

An important part of a democracy is the guarantee of freedom of dissent; people in a democracy can express their opinions openly even if they do not agree with established views.

NONSENSE

Without sense, words or actions that are foolish.

Some people believe that astrology helps tell the future, and some people think it is just a lot of nonsense.

SENSITIVE

Keenly aware.

The mother is very sensitive to her baby's feelings and needs.

Easily hurt.

You have to be careful about correcting Mary because she is very sensitive and cries easily.

Responsive to.

The artist is very sensitive to light and color.

PRESENTIMENT

A feeling that something, especially something evil, is about to happen, a foreboding.

When her son went into the army, she had a presentiment that he would be killed in the war.

SENTIMENT

What and how you feel about something.

His sentiment against racial prejudice is very strong.

SEND

To cause or enable to go.

They sent their son to camp for the summer.

To dispatch.

The Red Cross sent emergency supplies to the victims of the flood.

SENSIBLE

Intelligent, reasonable, showing good judgment.

Johnny was very sensible and did not ask for things his parents couldn't afford.

RESENT

To feel offended or angry from a sense of injury or insult.

Mary resented always having to babysit for her kid brother.

CONSENT

To feel with, to agree, to give permission.

Father finally gave his consent to the marriage arrangements.

SENSUAL

Connection with physical or sexual pleasure, voluptuous.

He considered her long dark hair sensual.

ASSENT

To agree, to concur, to feel or think with.

The strike ended when both sides assented to the terms.

SENSUOUS

Having a strong effect on the senses.

The melodic music was very sensuous.

S E Q U

Meaning: To follow.

Origin: Latin, *sequi*, to follow.
French, *suivre*, to follow
("qu" drops out in French).

An interesting member of this family is the word EXECUTE. The word literally means *to follow out*. Thus, EXECUTE came to mean *to carry out a death sentence*.

The word also has a less unpleasant meaning, which is *to carry out a plan*, or *to perform*. In this sense we say: "The architect's plan was *executed* in every detail;" or "The ballet dancer *executed* a leap that made the audience cheer."

Although the verb form of the word EXECUTE does not distinguish between its various meanings, the noun forms of the word do. A person who carries out a death penalty is an EXECUTIONER; a person who sees that plans are carried out is an EXECUTIVE; and a person who specifically carries out the provisions of a will is an EXECUTOR.

PROSECUTE

To bring before a court of law, to follow up.

After passing many false checks, he was prosecuted for forgery.

SUITE

A group of connected rooms.

They rented the bridal suite for their wedding.

A set of matched furniture.

They bought a dining room suite for their new apartment.

A musical composition that follows a certain form.

The musicians were applauded for their playing of Tchaikowsky's "Nutcracker Suite."

SUITOR

A wooer, a man who follows ardently after a woman.

The beautiful young girl has many suitors.

SEQUENCE

Order, one thing following another.

All the boys in the family followed the same sequence of going to college, marrying, and going into the family business.

CONSEQUENCE

Something that follows after another event, a result.

He did not do his homework all semester long and as a consequence he failed the final exam.

CONSECUTIVE

Following in order or succession, without interruption.

He was out of work for three consecutive weeks and was getting very worried about his finances.

PERSECUTE

To pursue, to chase with a desire to hurt, to treat badly, to punish for religious or racial reasons.

All through history, minority groups such as the Jews, the Blacks, and the Armenians have been persecuted by being deprived of their rights and even of their lives.

NON SEQUITUR

A conclusion that does not follow logically.

Socrates is a man. Socrates has brown hair. Men have brown hair. (The third sentence is a non sequitur.)

INCONSEQUENTIAL

Unimportant, not following logically.

She tried to take her husband's mind off his troubles by chatting about inconsequential matters.

SUE

To take action in a court of law, to make a logical claim.

The landlord sued the tenant for not paying his rent.

PURSUE

To follow.

She pursued her goal of becoming a ballet dancer with great determination.

To chase.

The robbers got into their car and the cops pursued them, with guns blazing.

ENSUE

To follow immediately, to come afterward.

The employer and employees could not come to an agreement and a strike ensued.

SEQUEL

What follows as a result of.

A sequel to the Watergate affair was the resignation of President Nixon.

A continuation.

The Godfather II *was a sequel to the very successful movie based on Mario Puzo's book.*

SUITABLE

Fitting the purpose, proper.

She was worried that her simple dress would not be suitable for the formal party.

S I G N

Meaning: A distinguishing mark, a signal.

Origin: Latin, *signum*, a sign.

In days of old, SIGNET-rings served a very important function. The king, or a noble, would have his signature or symbol engraved on a ring. When the ring was pressed down on wax or clay, it left a very clear impression. Important papers were not valid unless they were sealed with the stamp from a signet ring. Although most common people could not read or write, they all recognized the king's seal, and thus knew the importance of a missive which bore that wax impression.

INSIGNIA

Badge, emblem which marks rank or membership.

The caduceus, with two serpents entwined about a winged staff, is the insignia of the medical profession.

SIGNAL

A sign agreed upon.

All over the world, a red light is a signal that means stop.

DESIGN

A plan, a purpose or intention.

*The hostess seated the eligible
bachelor next to the young
widow by design.*

DESIGN

A pattern.

*She picked a fabric with a
floral design for her sofa.*

SIGNATURE

A person's name written by
himself.

*John Hancock's signature on
the Declaration of Independence was large and bold. He
said, "I want King George to
be able to read this without his
spectacles."*

RESIGN

To give up or surrender an
office.

*The chairman resigned his
office because of ill health.*

To accept.

*Mary found it hard to resign
herself to the fact that her
romance was over.*

DESIGNATE

To mark out, to name for
office.

*Mahatma Gandhi designated
Nehru as his successor.*

ASSIGN

To sign over to, to appoint or
designate, to give out a task.

*Mary was assigned the job of
washing the blackboards.*

SIGNIFICANT

Important, full of meaning.

Losing thirty pounds made a significant change in her appearance.

CONSIGN

To hand over, to deliver goods to be sold.

The shipment of books was consigned to the university bookstore.

SIGNIFY

To be a sign of, to indicate.

The chairman asked all those who were in favor of the proposal to signify by raising their right hands.

To mean.

Even after we saw the movie, we didn't understand what the title signified.

S I S T

Meaning: To stand.

Origin: Latin, *sistere*, to stand.

It took millions of years of evolution for a species to develop that could stand and walk erect. Standing up means more than being erect. When you stand up to your enemies, or for your rights, you exhibit your stature and strength, and in effect, the power of your personality.

Many of the words derived from the root "sist" preserve this thought.

CONSISTENT

Keeping with the same ideas or behavior.

John is consistent: he is late for work every single morning.

In agreement with.

The professor's conservative ideas about politics are not consistent with his liberal ideas about education.

PERSIST

To continue standing up against all odds, to refuse to give up.

Mary persisted in wearing her sister's clothes no matter how many times she was punished for it.

CONSIST

To stand together, to be made up of.

The dinner consisted of soup, chicken, rice, carrots, salad, and dessert.

DESIST

To stand back from, to stop

The taxi driver desisted from blowing his horn when the police appeared.

ASSIST

To stand by, to help.

Mary assisted her mother with the cooking by peeling the potatoes and onions.

RESIST

To stand up against, to oppose.

When the Nazis invaded Holland, many of the Dutch people resisted them.

ASSISTANT

A person who helps; a person who serves in a lower rank.

The nurse is an excellent assistant to the doctor.

INSIST

To stand up for, to demand strongly.

Mary's parents insist that she be home before midnight when she goes out on a date.

S O L V   S O L U

Meaning: To loosen, to unbind, to explain, to clear up.

Origin: Latin, *solvere*, to loosen, to free.

The democratic ideal is a relatively new concept in human relations. For thousands of years, the power of the ruler was ABSOLUTE and unlimited. As Pharaoh said to Joseph, "I am Pharaoh, and without me no man can raise his hand in all Egypt."

The kings of Israel shared the tradition of the times and upheld the absolute rule of the king. However, the Hebrew religious ideal found this belief offensive, as illustrated in the following story:

King Ahab of Israel wanted to buy the vineyard of Naboth, but Naboth refused to sell his vineyard. So the king had Naboth falsely charged and stoned to death.

The prophet Elijah heard what the king had done. In a burst of fury, he came before the king, cursed him bitterly, and forecast the downfall of his dynasty: "You have murdered and you think you will take possession; where the dogs have licked the blood of Naboth they will also lick yours."

A mighty challenge to absolutism!

SOLVENT

Able to pay one's debts.

He was heavily in debt, but became solvent when he received the inheritance from his uncle.

A substance used for dissolving another substance.

Benzine is a solvent used in dry cleaning to remove oil stains.

SOLUBLE

Able to be explained.

The problem is difficult, but with a little patience it is soluble.

Capable of being melted or dissolved.

She used water-soluble glue to mend the cup and it came apart again in the dishwater.

SOLUTION

An explanation.

To find the solution to the problem of why the apple fell on his head, Newton worked out his famous law of gravity.

SOLUTION

A liquid mixture.

She bathed the dog's sore paw in a solution of boric acid and water.

ABSOLVE

To free from guilt or blame.

After the investigation, the suspect was absolved from any involvement in the murder.

ABSOLUTE

Free from restriction or quali-fication, complete.

When giving evidence in a law court, we must tell the abso-lute truth.

SOLVE

To explain, to clear up, to find the answer to.

Sherlock Holmes solved many mysterious murders.

DISSOLVE

To loosen the parts, to melt or diffuse in liquid.

The sugar dissolved in the hot tea.

RESOLUTION

A decision or a determination.

My New Year's resolution will be to give up smoking.

RESOLUTE

Determined, firm.

He was resolute in his deci-sion to stop smoking.

DISSOLUTE

Wicked, with loose morals.

*Henry VIII led a dissolute life
and had six wives, two of
whom he had beheaded.*

S P E C

Meaning: To see; to look.

Origin: Latin, *specere*, to see.
Latin, *spectare*, to behold.

From 1711-1712, Joseph Addison and Richard Steele published in England a journal entitled the *Spectator*. Its essays, written by imaginary members of the Spectator Club, offered trenchant comments on the manners, morals, and religion of the times.

A SPECTATOR, or *onlooker,* who observes people or events from the outside may render a more objective account than someone who is a direct participant.

CONSPICUOUS

Easy to see, obvious, attracting attention.

His casual clothes made him very conspicuous at a party where everyone else was dressed formally.

INSPECTOR

An official examiner; an officer on the police force.

After the fire, the health, police, and fire inspectors all came to examine the ruined premises.

DESPICABLE

Worthy of being looked down on, contemptible.

Robbing and killing the old man was a despicable act.

CIRCUMSPECT

Looking carefully at everything that relates to the matter at hand, taking everything into account, cautious.

The employer was very circumspect about firing the employee who had been accused of theft, and he carefully examined all the evidence before coming to a conclusion.

SPECIMEN

A sample to look at, a part used as an example of the whole, a typical part used for scientific examination.

The botanist collected specimens of every kind of butterfly.

SPECULATE

To look at or think about different aspects or possibilities; to take part in a risky business venture in the hopes of making a large profit.

Having ended up penniless, he often speculated about what might have happened to him had he not used his entire fortune to speculate in the stock market.

PERSPECTIVE

A view that puts things in proper relation to each other, an evaluation that gives proportional importance to the various parts of the whole.

Often when one is in the midst of a situation, one does not have the perspective of another who views the matter from a distance.

SPECTACULAR

Unusual or striking looking.

There was a spectacular show of fireworks in honor of Independence Day.

RESPECT

To look up to, to show consideration or esteem for, a feeling of courteous regard for.

Children are always being reminded to respect their elders.

In relation to.

He didn't want to hurt her feelings and found it hard to express his real opinion with respect to her plans.

SPECTACLE

A strange or remarkable display, a public show, an unusual sight; a pair of eyeglasses to improve vision.

He put on his spectacles so that he might be better able to view the spectacle of the beauty parade.

SPECTER

A ghostly apparition.

Clad in gray chiffon, she glided silently through the room like a specter.

An object of fear or dread.

The specter of unemployment is plaguing the nation.

SPECTRUM

A series of color bands arranged in order of their wave lengths; the range of radio wave lengths.

There was not a single news broadcast to be heard at that particular hour on the entire radio spectrum.

PERSPICACITY

Keenness of sight, judgment, or understanding.

The child had been so close to his mother that he showed unusual perspicacity about her moods and wishes.

ASPECT

How something or someone looks, appearance from a specific view.

One's ideas about justice may differ depending on whether one is viewing crime from the aspect of the criminal or from the aspect of the victim.

RETROSPECT

A looking back at things of the past.

When they discussed the accident they realized in retrospect that there were many things they might have done to avoid it.

S P I R E

Meaning: To breathe.

Origin: Latin, *spirare*, to breathe.

RESPIRATION is *breathing in and out*. Without breath, there is no life. Some of the words that have ''spire'' as their root touch the cycle of life.

For example, EXPIRE means *to breathe out,* and it also means *to die*. Some people believe that when you expire, your SPIRIT, or *soul*, leaves the body.

TRANSPIRE

To breathe across or out. Originally the meaning was to leak out, to escape from secrecy to public notice; today the common meaning is to happen, to turn out.

We do not know what transpired at the secret meeting between the foreign ministers, but there is much curiosity about it.

CONSPIRACY

Literally breathing together, plotting together, usually for unlawful purposes.

The husband was running around with other women, but there was a conspiracy of silence and nobody told the wife.

ASPIRE

To breathe toward, to have a desire for, an ambition for.

John has decided to study law because he aspires to hold an important office in government.

RESPIRATION

Breathing in and out.

In the process of respiration, people take in oxygen and breathe out carbon dioxide, while plants do the opposite.

SPRIGHTLY

Animated, lively, full of spirit.

Although she was 80 years old, she was sprightly and still enjoyed a parade.

PERSPIRE

Literally to breathe through; to sweat.

The elevator was crowded and hot, and soon everyone began to perspire heavily.

INSPIRE

To breathe in or inhale.

When the doctor was checking her lungs, he told her to inspire deeply.

To arouse religious or divine feeling.

The minister's sermon would always inspire his congregation.

To stimulate, to have an exalting influence upon.

Reading about the life of Helen Keller inspired Mary to become a teacher.

EXPIRE

To breathe out.

The dog expires very heavily in his sleep.

To die.

The British novelist George Orwell requested that when he expired his grave be marked with his real name, Eric Arthur Blair.

To terminate, come to an end.

Our lease expires in two months and then we will move to another apartment.

SPIRIT

Frame of mind, mood.

The Christmas spirit was everywhere and people were feeling gay and generous.

Courage, cheer, enthusiasm, loyalty.

The new principal was respected and liked by everyone, and school spirit was high.

Phantom, ghost.

My grandmother goes to seances to try to communicate with the spirit of her dead husband.

ESPRIT DE CORPS

Group spirit, the morale of the group.

With each victory in a local election, the esprit de corps of the political campaigners rose higher and higher.

SPRITE

Pixie, fairy, elf.

The children ran across the grass like sprites.

S T A

Meaning: To stand.

Origin: Latin, *stare*, to stand.

Greek, *stasis*, standing.

In St. Peter's Church in Rome, there is a beautiful statue of Moses, which was sculpted by Michelangelo in the sixteenth century.

Why has the great artist put two horns on Moses' head? Thereby hangs a tale—a linguistic tale:

The Hebrew Bible says that when Moses came down from Mt. Sinai carrying the Ten Commandments, "the skin of his face shone." In Hebrew, the word "keren" means *shone,* but it also means *a horn,* because the ancient Hebrews described the rays of the sun as horns.

When St. Jerome translated the Hebrew Bible into Latin, he mistranslated this verse, writing, "horns formed on Moses' head." The translation should have been, "rays shone from Moses' head."

STABILITY

The ability to stand and not topple over, steadiness, firmness of character.

It is a great blessing for parents if their children have stability and are not influenced by every passing fad.

APOSTATE

Literally one who stands away from his faith, who gives up his faith.

The Roman emperor Julian is called Julian the Apostate because he gave up the Christian faith and tried to restore paganism.

STABLE

A place where horses stand, a building where horses are sheltered.

The horses were led into the stable.

STABLE

Firm, not easily moved or thrown off balance.

One of its legs was shorter than the others so the table was not very stable.

STATURE

The way a person stands, height; physical, mental or moral growth.

Most basketball players are well above average stature.

Standing, merit.

When his book was published, his stature in his profession rose.

STATIONERY

Materials for writing letters; paper, envelopes, cards, etc. Originally, a stationer was a bookseller or publisher, or a tradesman who stood still and had a fixed station or shop.

Mary stopped at the stationery store to get a birthday card for her friend.

STAY

To stand still, to remain.

She had to stay in bed for a week after her operation.

To live for a while.

The children stayed with their grandparents while their parents were on a vacation trip.

ARMISTICE

Literally, the arms standing still, an agreement to stop the fighting.

The Armistice on November 11th, 1918, ending World War I, brought wild rejoicing to all the world.

STATION

A place where someone stands or is located.

When John first went into the army he was stationed near his home.

The regular stopping place of a bus or train.

His wife picks him up at the railroad station when he comes home from work.

Social standing.

As president of his company he had reached a very important station in life.

OBSTETRICIAN

A doctor who specializes in treating women before and during childbirth—literally, one who stands by the woman.

The obstetrician told the pregnant woman that she would have twins.

THERMOSTAT

A device that controls the heat, making it stand still when a certain temperature has been reached.

Something was wrong with the thermostat and the house was overheated.

STATE

The way things stand, condition.

He was in a very bad state of mind after his divorce.

A nation, territory, or government.

Driving at excessive speed is prohibited by state law.

To tell in speech or writing.

In his inaugural address in March, 1933, Franklin D. Roosevelt stated, "The only thing we have to fear is fear itself."

CONSTANT

Remaining the same, not changing, stable.

Through all the years of struggle and hardship, their love remained constant.

Going on all the time, continual.

They could not finish their work because of the constant interruptions.

INSTANT

A short space of time, a moment.

It only took a few instants to empty the building after the fire alarm sounded.

Immediate, without delay.

He knew the matter was urgent and gave it his instant attention.

DISTANCE

Literally, standing apart, the space between two points.

They do not see each other very often because they live a great distance from one another.

STATIC

Standing still, not moving or progressing.

The professor felt it was time to change jobs because his career had been static for a long time.

Certain electrical discharges.

The storm produced a lot of static interference on the radio.

STATUS

Legal standing, position, rank.

She felt that her status as a divorcee imposed many disadvantages.

STATUTE

A standing rule or law.

The statutes with regard to divorce have been changing in recent years.

DISTANT

Standing far away from, far apart, widely separated.

The wedding hall was filled with family, friends, and a sprinkling of distant relatives.

ESTATE

Landed property.

The great estates of the nobility were taken over by the peasantry after the French Revolution.

STATISTICS

Facts that show how things stand.

Statistics show a sharp rise in the suicide rate among college students in the U.S. in recent years.

STATIONARY

Standing still, not changing.

The population of the town remained stationary for many years.

STRUCT

Meaning: To build.

Origin: Latin, *struere*, to build, to pile up.

When ancient man stopped residing in caves, he began to build more comfortable homes. The building of STRUCTURES of one sort or another has always preoccupied man on his long road towards civilized life.

The Egyptian pyramids were probably the most imposing single group of structures of the ancient world. The stone pyramids served as tombs for the mummified bodies of the pharaohs. The Great Pyramid of Cheops at Gizeh is one of the seven wonders of the world.

DESTROY

To tear down.

Many homes were destroyed by the flood.

To put an end to, to do away with.

Failing the examination destroyed all his hopes of going to college.

To kill.

The drought destroyed all the crops and created a danger of famine.

CONSTRUCTIVE

Building up, leading to improvement, positive.

The editor turned down the manuscript, but he made several constructive suggestions about how the author could improve it.

INSTRUMENT

Originally a tool with which you build; an implement with which people work.

The eye doctor used a special instrument to examine the patient's eyes.

INSTRUMENT

A means.

The bank robber used hostages as instruments for his escape.

INSTRUMENT

A device for making music.

Mary's favorite instrument is the flute.

INSTRUCT

To impart knowledge, to build up mentally, to teach.

His father instructed him in the ways of the business, and eventually he was able to run it by himself.

To give directions or orders.

Her mother instructed her never to open the door to strangers.

MISCONSTRUE

To interpret wrongly, to mis-understand.

The dog misconstrued the man's gesture as an attack on his master and barked fiercely.

CONSTRUCT

To put together, to build.

The most beautiful building in the world, the Taj Mahal, was constructed in Agra, India, by Shah Jahan as a memorial for his favorite wife.

OBSTRUCT

To pile up and block, to hinder.

We used to be able to see Mt. Scopus from our window, but then a new building went up which obstructed our view.

SUME   SUMP

Meaning: To take.

Origin: Latin, *sumere*, to take.

The word PRESUME, which means *to take for granted,* was made world famous by Henry Stanley. Everyone has heard the now famous expression uttered by Stanley when he encountered Livingstone in the trackless wilds of the African forest, ''Dr. Livingstone, I presume.''

David Livingstone was a medical missionary and explorer in Africa. One of the first white men to travel in the unknown continent, Livingstone made many groundbreaking discoveries. Then, accounts of his journey ceased, and the world lost track of him.

Born in Wales as John Rowlands, Henry Stanley took the name of his adoptive father when he came to America to live. He covered the Civil War as a journalist for the New York *Herald.* The newspaper later commissioned him to search for David Livingstone.

Stanley found Livingstone, ill and run-down, at Ujiji on Lake Tanganyika, on November 10, 1871. The masterpiece of understatement with which he greeted the great explorer will long be remembered.

CONSUMPTION

Using up.

The consumption of eggs has been decreasing in the United States.

A disease that causes the lungs to waste away, tuberculosis.

The heroine of the opera La Traviata *suffered from consumption.*

PRESUME

To take for granted.

The doctor presumed that the patient had been taking the medicine he had given him.

To take liberties.

She presumed upon their friendship to ask him to use his influence to get her a job.

ASSUME

To take to oneself, usurp.

When the child started to cry, the grandmother assumed charge, ignoring the mother completely.

To take for granted.

Mary assumed that she would be invited to her cousin's wedding and bought a new dress for the affair.

RESUME

To take back, to begin again

After the strike was settled, sanitation service was resumed and the garbage began to disappear from the streets.

Summary. (French, with accent on first and third syllables.)

In his book report, he gave a résumé of the plot and criticised the author's style.

PRESUMPTUOUS

Taking too much for granted, too bold.

Mary thought it was presumptuous of John to come to the party when he had not been invited.

CONSUMER

A person who uses up goods or services.

Today there are many publications that help the consumer choose the best product at the best price.

CONSUME

To use up.

My new car gives me good mileage and consumes much less gas than my old car.

To eat or drink up.

The average American consumes about 525 pounds of food a year.

To be filled with.

She was consumed with anxiety about the letter her mother got from her teacher.

T E L

Meaning: Far away.

Origin: Greek, *tele*, far away.

The word root "tel" is a monument to man's mastery over distance. Throughout the course of history, man has invented some of the most sophisticated devices imaginable in order to maintain contact with his fellowman.

Many years ago, the fastest way to send a message was by a swift horse or by a swift runner. Other means of communication were smoke and sun signals, sent from mountain top to mountain top, or birds trained to carry messages. For thousands of years, there was no change, as no new methods of communication were devised.

Hammurabi, King of Babylon in 2200 B.C., could get a message to one of his generals just as rapidly as could George Washington.

The battle of New Orleans, in which Jackson defeated the British, was actually fought in vain. By January 1815, the War of 1812 had already ended, but word had not yet reached the distant city of New Orleans by the time the battle was fought.

Samuel F.B. Morse perfected a method of using electrical current for purposes of communication. Using the fact that a light flashes when an electric current is interrupted, he devised a system that used these flashes to stand for the letters of the alphabet.

After twelve years of hard work, the first crude TELEGRAPH employing the Morse code was perfected. In 1844, to demonstrate his magical new instrument to Congress, Morse sent the famous message "What hath God wrought!" over a wire from Washington to Baltimore.

TELEPHONE

An instrument for conveying sound over distances

In 1876, Alexander Bell exhibited the first perfected telephone at the centennial in Philadelphia.

TELEVISION

An instrument for conveying images or scenes over long distances.

In the fifty years since television was invented, it has spread to all parts of the world.

TELEPROMPTER

A device that enables a television speaker to see the words of his speech in large letters before him.

The teleprompter makes a prepared speech sound spontaneous instead of memorized.

TELSTAR

A communication satellite which receives signals from one part of the globe and sends them on to another.

Telstar enables live news events to be viewed immediately all around the world.

TELEPHOTO

A picture of things that are very far away.

The heavenly bodies can be photographed by a camera with a telephoto lens.

TEN

Meaning: To hold.

Origin: Latin, *tenere*, to hold.

One of the qualities that has enabled man to survive against all obstacles is TENACITY, *the ability to hold fast and firm, to be persistent and stubborn.*

One of the most striking examples of human tenacity is the invention of modern lighting.

Man has always longed for light; darkness signifies gloom, fear, uncertainty. Fire was the first source of light. The first lamp was a dish with oil and a wick. Then came the candle, the lantern, and the kerosene lamp.

It took some time before the power of electricity could be put to practical use. It was known to exist in the lightning that flashed in the sky. Benjamin Franklin teased electricity out of the heavens with a flying kite.

In 1879, Thomas Alva Edison patented the incandescent lamp. With very little change, this is the lamp that lights up our world.

Then the neon light was invented for commercial signs. Advertisements, aglow in neon lights, have changed the face of many a large city.

CONTAIN

To hold together, to include.

The chest contained many old maps and documents, some old coins and books.

CONTAIN

To control.

When the doctor told him his wife had given birth to a boy, he couldn't contain himself and jumped up and down for joy.

CONTINENT

One of the six large land masses of the earth.

The continents of Africa and Asia have the highest birth rates in the world.

LIEUTENANT

One who takes the place of someone else.

In New York State, the lieutenant governor takes over when the governor is ill.

A ranking officer in the Army.

The sergeant was promoted to lieutenant for his excellent command of the platoon.

ABSTAIN

To hold off, to voluntarily keep away from.

The doctor told the patient to abstain from alcohol and tobacco.

MAINTAIN

Literally to hold onto, to keep up.

It is hard to maintain your usual standard of living with costs rising so sharply.

To declare to be true, to assert.

The accused maintained that he had not stolen the watch but had bought it in a second-hand shop.

ABSTENTION

Holding back, refraining.

There were thirty votes in favor of the resolution, fourteen against, and three abstentions.

CONTAINER

A box, jar, can, or carton that holds something.

Whenever the children visit us, we have to remember to buy extra containers of milk.

RETENTIVE

Having a good memory.

The child is very retentive and remembers everything he learns.

DETAIN

To hold back, to keep in custody.

The policeman detained the suspect in order to question him further.

To keep from going on, to delay.

John was late for his appointment because he was detained by heavy traffic.

INCONTINENT

Unable to hold back the natural discharge of urine.

When the old woman became incontinent, her children had to put her in a nursing home.

TENABLE

Capable of being held or defended.

Her belief may be tenable, but not many individuals would want to test it.

SUSTENANCE

Food, nourishment, means of support.

The invalid's only sustenance was the food brought in by his neighbor.

ABSTINENCE

Keeping away from food, drink, or other pleasures.

He tried to cut down on his smoking, but he realized that the only way he would succeed in breaking his habit was through total abstinence.

TENURE

Holding or possessing something.

The tenure of the office of the Presidency in the United States is four years.

RETAIN

To hold back, to keep.

When they were divorced, the wife retained the children.

SUSTAIN

To keep going, to support or uphold.

What sustained her after the news that her husband had been arrested was her belief in his innocence.

TENANT

One who holds on, one who occupies land or a house in return for a rental.

The tenants complained to the landlord that they were not getting enough heat.

T E N D

Meaning: To stretch.

Origin: Latin, *tendere*, to stretch, to reach.

A word which has become popular in newspaper reports these days is DÉTENTE. Literally, the word means *to unstretch*. The policy of détente in international affairs is designed to lessen the tensions between countries.

With the advent of the atomic bomb, détente seems to be the chief hope for peace. Unless the great powers of the world can work out some way of co-existing peacefully, humanity is in grave danger of rendering itself extinct.

CONTEND

To stretch out with all one's strength, to strive, to struggle, to compete.

The teacher asked to be assigned to a different school because he could not contend with the behavior problems of his students.

To argue, to assert as true.

Copernicus contended that the earth moved around the sun and was not the center of the universe.

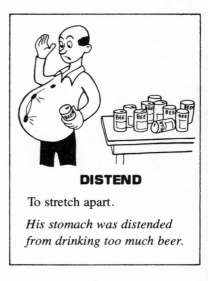

DISTEND

To stretch apart.

His stomach was distended from drinking too much beer.

INTENSE

Very strong.

He went to see the doctor because he had intense pain in his chest.

ATTEND

To be present at, to go to.

Despite the bad weather, many people attended the meeting.

TENT

A stretched-out cloth or skin structure used as a portable shelter.

Their tent had several holes in it and they were very uncomfortable when it rained during their camping trip.

ATTENTION

Stretching toward, listening to, observing carefully.

The sign said to keep off the grass, but no one paid any attention to it.

INTEND

To have in mind, to plan.

She intended to visit her grandmother after she finished her homework, but she didn't get through in time.

INTENSIFY

To make stronger.

He intensified his efforts in order to finish all his work before he went on vacation.

ATTENDANCE

Being present.

The child was ill a great deal and his school attendance was poor.

Number of people present.

The attendance at the meeting was very poor due to the snow storm.

EXTENT

How far something stretches; degree, scope.

His tennis had improved to some extent, but he still had a long way to go before becoming a really good player.

EXTEND

To stretch out, to continue.

The line of cars waiting to pay the toll extended for a mile.

To enlarge, prolong.

We were having such a good time that we decided to extend our vacation for another week.

To offer.

The professor extended an invitation to all his students to meet at his home for informal discussion.

PORTEND

To stretch forth, to be a sign of, to be a warning.

Brisk winds portend a stormy sea.

TENDENCY

Leaning toward, inclination to act in a certain way.

John has a tendency to drive too fast whether or not he is in a hurry.

TENDER

To offer, to stretch out to.

He wasn't very happy with his job so he tendered his resignation.

THIN

Slender, narrow.

Although John is thin, he is very strong and healthy.

TENUOUS

Slight, flimsy.

The young teacher was inexperienced and her control over the class was tenuous.

TENSE

Stretched out, showing nervous strain.

All of us were very tense as we waited for the election results.

PRETEND

To stretch before, to make believe, to claim falsely.

The child dressed up in his cowboy outfit and pretended he was in the rodeo.

INTENT, INTENTION

Stretching toward, what one aims to do.

There is a cynical proverb which says, "The road to hell is paved with good intentions."

EXTENSIVE

Stretched out, far-reaching, comprehensive.

They bought an old house and had to make extensive repairs before they could move in.

THESIS

Meaning: To put, to place.

Origin: Greek, *tithenai*, to put, to place.

In general, nature supplies whatever man needs in the way of food or materials for clothing. But man has attempted to improve upon nature by producing large numbers of SYNTHETIC materials. These materials are produced chemically by man, and not by nature. There are synthetic dyes, synthetic fabrics, and even synthetic food products.

But it is hard to exceed the perfection or beauty of natural things. Although man's fantastic synthetic creations speak well of his skill and ingenuity, they often create as many problems as they solve. Synthetics confuse nature's delicate balance, and may harm our natural environment.

SYNTHESIS

Putting parts together into wholes.

The historical novel achieved a remarkable synthesis of fact and imagination.

ANTITHESIS

Putting something against.

With his gentle personality, he was the antithesis of his aggressive older brother.

THEME

What is put down, a topic or subject.

The professor delivered a very interesting lecture on the theme of zero population growth.

METATHESIS

To transpose or change the order of sounds in a word.

The word bird *developed from old English by metathesis from the original word* brid.

APOTHECARY

Originally, a storekeeper who would put his goods away in an orderly fashion, a druggist, pharmacist.

He took the prescription his doctor gave him to the apothecary to be filled.

THESAURUS

Literally, where one stores or puts things, a treasury of words.

Roget's Thesaurus is a very valuable reference book giving synonyms and antonyms of many English words.

THESIS

What one states or puts down, an essay, a proposition to be proved.

His thesis for his doctoral degree was about the grammatical vs. the conversational methods of foreign-language teaching.

PARENTHESIS

An insertion beside, an additional explanatory remark; one of the two curved marks enclosing a parenthetical expression.

The full name of the company was given as a parenthesis after the initials, as TWA (Trans World Airlines).

HYPOTHESIS

Literally, placing under, a theory or assumption, a tentative explanation.

The cancer research center is trying to test the hypothesis that some forms of cancer are caused by viruses.

WORDS COME IN FAMILIES   311

TREASURE

Valuable things, riches.

She considers her children her greatest treasure.

To value highly.

She treasures the first letter she ever got from her son.

EPITHET

Literally, to put upon, a descriptive word or name.

King Richard I of England won the epithet Richard the Lion-Hearted for his warrior activity in the Crusades.

T H E O S

Meaning: God.

Origin: Greek, *theos*, God.

There was a time when all men worshipped idols, believing that the graven images had great power over their lives. People brought gifts to appease the gods represented by the idols, and they made sacrifices to them. Sometimes, even human beings were sacrificed to honor the idols.

Then Abraham, the father of the Hebrew people, conceived of one, invisible, all-powerful God of all the world. Abraham taught this belief of MONOTHEISM to his children and to his children's children.

In the 10th century B.C., King Solomon built the first temple in Jerusalem. For about a thousand years, the temple served as a center of worship of the one invisible God—a tiny island surrounded by a sea of idol worship.

The hold of idolatry was finally loosened under the influence of Christianity which spread monotheism throughout Europe and Asia.

THEOLOGY

The study of God and of religious doctrines.

Students for the priesthood spend many years studying theology.

THEODORE

This name means the gift of God.

They named the baby Theodore, but everyone called him Teddy.

POLYTHEISM

The worship of many gods.

Many myths about gods and goddesses have come down to us from the polytheism of ancient Greece.

ENTHUSIASM

Inspired by, or filled with, the spirit of God; strong interest, eagerness.

The mountain climber was filled with enthusiasm as he made his way to the mountain peak.

ATHEISM

The belief that there is no God.

The religious father deplored his son's atheism.

T O M Y

Meaning: Cut, cutting

Origin: Greek, *temnein*, to cut.

Greek, *tomos*, cutting.

Possibly the most important fact of modern life is the existence of the ATOM bomb. The bomb hangs over us all as a threat which cannot be ignored.

Originally, all the energy on earth came from the sun. The ultimate source of wood, coal, gas, oil, and the electricity made from these fuels, is the light and heat poured forth from the sun since the beginning of time.

Then Albert Einstein devised the famous formula in which he described the enormous energy locked up in the atom, a particle so small as not to be divisible. Einstein predicted that, for the first time in history, man would be able to use energy that did not come from the sun.

Other scientists began to develop ways and means of splitting the atom. When they succeeded, a terrible power was unleashed.

With the world at the mercy of Adolf Hitler, Einstein wrote to President Roosevelt urging that the United States develop the atom bomb. The physicist argued that if America did not develop the bomb first, Germany would.

On August 6, 1945, the first atom bomb ever used in warfare was dropped on Hiroshima, virtually destroying the Japanese city. President Truman justified the use of the bomb by pointing out that it brought World War II to an abrupt end, saving many more lives than it destroyed.

Today, we face life with the atom bomb, a force for evil, and atomic energy, a potential source for good. What political forces will determine the direction humanity will take?

ANATOMY

The cutting up or dissection of a plant or animal, the science of the structure of plants and animals.

Models of the human organs are very useful for students who are studying anatomy.

ATOMIZER

A device for breaking up and spraying particles of perfume.

She always smells good because she keeps an atomizer in her purse and uses it frequently.

TONSILLECTOMY

Operation to remove the tonsils.

In the past, a tonsillectomy was performed routinely when a child had infected tonsils, but today this operation is less common.

APPENDECTOMY

The cutting out of the appendix.

She complained of a pain in her side and when the doctor examined her he rushed her to the hospital for an appendectomy.

MASTECTOMY

Surgical removal of a breast.

Doctors are trying to find treatments other than mastectomy for cancer of the breast.

TOME

A volume of a literary work, a large or heavy book.

He is interested in American history and has read many tomes on the Civil War.

HYSTERECTOMY

Surgical removal of the uterus.

Many middle-aged women undergo hysterectomies to avoid the spread of cancer from the uterus to other parts of the body.

EPITOME

Literally, cut short, something or some part that is typical or representative.

His graduation speech was the epitome of wisdom and wit.

ENTOMOLOGY

The science of insects—literally, notched or cut animals.

The teacher brought in a book on entomology so the children could identify the bug they found in their classroom.

TORT

Meaning: To twist.

Origin: Latin, *torquere*, to twist.

The most common word which has the root "tort" does not, strictly speaking, belong to this family. The TORTOISE or TURTLE has made

its way into this family of words through folk etymology.

The ancient Greeks believed that the tortoise was a demon; the word TORTOISE derives from "Tartarus," *an animal from the infernal regions*. Later, the twisted legs of the tortoise caused the word to be associated with the Latin root "tort."

TORTURE

Inflicting severe mental or physical pain on someone in order to punish him or force him to confess or give information.

The prisoner accused the police of torturing him in order to make him confess.

TORSION

The tendency of a twisted cord, wire, or bar to return to its untwisted position.

The torsion balance is an instrument which helps to test how well materials used as rotating parts in machines can resist twisting.

DISTORT

To twist out of shape.

When he was hit by the bullet, the soldier's face distorted with pain.

To misstate, to misrepresent, to twist the facts.

Mary's description of her quarrel with John distorted the facts and made it sound as though it were all John's fault.

EXTORT

To twist out, to get money by the use of force or threat.

Racketeers often extort money from a storekeepers by threatening them.

RETORT

To twist back, to answer sharply and quickly.

When Willie Sutton was asked why he robbed banks, he retorted, "Because that's where the money is."

CONTORTIONIST

A person who can twist his body in unusual ways.

Houdini, the world's most famous contortionist, was able to wriggle out of a straitjacket while loaded with iron shackles and ropes.

TORTILLA

Thin, flat, round, unleavened bread.

In Mexico you can often see the women twisting and turning the cornmeal dough to make tortillas.

TORTUOUS

Full of twists and turns.

The road through the mountains was tortuous and he had to drive slowly and carefully.

Crooked, not straightforward.

The course of their romance was tortuous, with many break-ups and make-ups, but it ended happily in marriage.

T R A C T

Meaning: To draw, to pull.

Origin: Latin, *trahere*, *tractus*, to draw.

In the mid-eighteenth century, the French philosopher, Jean Jacques Rousseau, published the *Social Contract*. In this work, he presented the idea that the powers of government rest in the people. He argued that when men leave their natural state to enter a more complex social organization, they retain their civic freedom by entering into a social contract together. The people agree to give powers to the rulers as long as they govern wisely and well. If the rulers do not fulfill their task, these powers may be re-assumed by the people.

At a time when absolute monarchs ruled over most of the world, the revolutionary ideas of the *Social Contract* helped form the philosophical basis for the American Revolution and the French Revolution. The idea of government by and for the governed became a powerful reality.

TRACTION

Pulling power or friction.

His car skidded because the tires were worn and had very little traction when the road was wet.

TRACTOR

A vehicle for pulling farm machinery.

The farmer bought a tractor to plow his land.

ATTRACTIVE

Drawing positive reactions, pleasing, pretty.

The attractive young girl attracted men as easily as a flower attracts bees.

DISTRACT

To draw away.

John distracted his mother's attention while his brother stole some cookies from the jar.

CONTRACT

A written formal agreement between people.

They were very nervous about signing the marriage contract.

To draw together, to reduce in size.

The pupil of the eye contracts when there is too much light.

To get, to acquire.

Her vacation was spoiled when she contracted poison ivy and had to put medication all over her arms and legs.

TRACE

A visible mark left by someone on something.

She recovered very rapidly and the only trace left from the accident was a small scar on her arm.

To follow the course of.

In his lecture, the professor traced the history of slavery from ancient to modern times.

To copy.

The boy traced the map by putting tissue paper over it.

TREAT

To handle; to behave toward a person or subject in a particular way.

John treats his grandparents with great affection and respect.

To consider, to regard.

When Mary forgot to take along the key to the suitcase, her husband treated it as a joke.

To try to relieve or cure.

The doctor said that the only way to treat a cold is with rest and lots of liquids.

To make a gift of food, drink, or entertainment.

On his birthday, John treated all his friends to ice-cream.

RETRACT

To withdraw.

The senator retracted the statement he had made opposing the foreign aid bill and said he would vote for it.

TRAIT

A quality or characteristic of personality.

The trait she admired most in him was his gentleness.

CONTRACTOR

A person who agrees to do certain work for a certain sum.

The building contractor said the house would be finished in June.

EXTRACT

To draw out, to put out

He dreaded going to the dentist because he knew he had to have two teeth extracted.

A passage taken from a book or speech.

The newspaper ran extracts from the President's speech covering the most important points he made about foreign policy.

TRACT

A stretch of land.

The tract of land he had bought became very valuable when the government built a road alongside it.

A system or part of the body with a special function.

Flu, or influenza, is a disease of the respiratory tract.

CONTRACTION

In grammar, the shortening of a word or phrase by the omission of letters.

Isn't *is a contraction for* is not.

TRACTABLE

Easy to manage, docile, compliant.

Many hyperactive children are given medication to sedate them and make them more tractable.

SUBTRACT

To draw or take away from.

The women who ran a cake sale found that after they subtracted their expenses they had not made much profit.

V A C

Meaning: To be vacant, empty, unoccupied.

Origin: Latin, *vacare*, to be empty, vacant.

It has been said that "nature abhors a VACUUM" or *empty space*. Indeed, a perfect vacuum has never been obtained. However, man has been successful in creating a partial vacuum by removing the molecules of gas or vapor from a confined space.

The sound you hear when a vacuum can or pump is used is usually identified as suction, but actually the suction caused by a vacuum is the pressure of the atmosphere rushing in to fill the unoccupied space.

The principle of the vacuum has many applications in the home, in industry and in scientific research—as, for example, in the vacuum cleaner, vacuum tube, and vacuum processing of food.

VACANCY

An opening, an unoccupied job or room.

During the Christmas season, all the hotels and motels were filled and there was not one vacancy.

AVOID

To keep away from.

The doctor told him to avoid foods with high fat because of his heart condition.

To get out of.

Mary always manages to avoid doing the dishes by claiming she has to do her homework.

DEVOID

Empty of, completely without.

After the death of his wife, the man felt that his life was devoid of meaning.

VOID

Ineffective, useless, having no legal force.

The contract was declared null and void because it was signed by a person under the legal age.

An empty space, a feeling of emptiness.

After his dog died, there was a void in his life.

VACUUM

Cleaner; a machine for cleaning carpets.

She was using the vacuum and did not hear the doorbell ring.

EQUIVALENT

Of equal value.

One cup of malted milk is equivalent in calories to a three-ounce hamburger.

VAIN

Worthless, futile.

All their attempts to locate their old friends were in vain; they simply could not find them.

Having a high regard for one's looks or ability, conceited.

She was very vain about her looks and was worried that her injury would leave a scar.

EVACUATE

To empty out or to remove the contents or occupants of, to withdraw.

During the blitz in London, many women and children were evacuated to country villages.

VACANT

Empty, having nothing in it.

The rent was very high and the apartment remained vacant for a long time.

VACUOUS

Empty of thought or interest,
stupid.

*He didn't know anything about
the subject and his conversation was completely vacuous.*

VACATION

A period of freedom from
work.

*They usually spend their sum-
mer vacation camping.*

VACATE

To make empty, to leave.

*Everybody was asked to va-
cate the building because of
the bomb scare.*

V A L

Meaning: To be strong, to be well, to possess worth.

Origin: Latin, *valere*, to be strong, to have power, to possess worth.

The word INVALID is actually two separate words. With the accent on the first syllable, INVALID means *someone who is infirm or disabled because of sickness or injury*. Franklin D. Roosevelt became an invalid when he was struck with polio.

With the second syllable accented, the word INVALID means *unlawful*. Forged documents are invalid. Checks that are over a year old are also invalid.

Of course, both these meanings are related to the root meaning. An invalid is not strong. Something that is invalid is not worth anything.

There are other pairs of words in English which are identical except for accent. As the accent changes, so does the meaning of the word and the part of speech it is. Here are a few examples:

con**duct**: lead

conduct: behavior

in**cense**: to anger

incense: substance giving sweet smell when burned

in**ter**: to bury

inter: between (prefix)

pre**sent**: to offer

present: now, here; a gift

pro**duce**: to create

produce: farm products

re**cord**: to write down

record: a report; a disk

re**sume**: to take up again

résumé: a summary

PREVAIL

To be the strongest, to gain the ascendancy, to succeed.

The two baseball teams were very good, but finally the Cardinals prevailed and won the game.

To persuade.

Although her father objected at first, Mary prevailed upon him to let her borrow his car for the evening.

VALUABLE

Highly prized, of great worth.

Mary took the ring to a jeweler to be appraised and was pleased to hear that it was very valuable.

PREVALENT

Widespread, common.

The prevalent idea that the world was flat was shown to be wrong when Magellan's ships completed the first voyage around the world in 1522.

VALIANT

Courageous, bold.

The valiant young man ran into the burning house and rescued the child from the fire.

CONVALESCENT

Growing stronger, gradually recovering health after illness; a person who is recovering from an illness.

Convalescents have to be careful not to engage in strenuous activities.

VALID

True, sound, having legal force.

He had a doctor's note to show that he had a valid reason to be absent.

VALEDICTORY

A farewell speech, especially at a graduation.

In his valedictory address, the student thanked all the teachers for their patience during the students' rebellious years.

VALUE

How much something is worth.

He was going to drop out of school, but his parents convinced him of the value of a college degree.

VALOR

Courage, especially in conflict.

His valor in battle was superb, but he was shy with women.

V E N

Meaning: To come.

Origin: Latin, *venire*, to come.

The history of man is the history of INVENTION. As each INVENTOR worked out the ramifications of his new idea, the life style—indeed, the very condition of human life—changed in some way.

Certainly one of the most important inventions of modern times was the airplane. For thousands of years, man had envied the flight of birds, wishing that he, too, could fly as swiftly and effortlessly. From the days of Leonardo da Vinci, man had tried to create wings that would enable him to take to the air.

And then, on a desolate beach in North Carolina on December 17, 1903, the Wright brothers sent up into the air what looked like a large, flying box. The first airplane stayed aloft for thirty seconds.

Man was no longer bound to the earth. The air age had begun. From that first, tiny, toylike airplane have developed the mighty jet planes that carry man to all the corners of the earth.

ADVENTURE

Coming upon some unexpected experience, a dangerous or exciting enterprise.

The American explorers Lewis and Clark met with many strange and hazardous adventures in their famous first expedition to the West Coast.

CONVENTION

Coming together, an assembly of members or delegates.

Every four years in the United States, the great political parties hold conventions to choose their candidates for President.

CONVENTIONAL

Customary, conforming with accepted rules, not original.

Mary did not want a conventional wedding with the usual ceremony and banquet, so she planned an informal, unconventional wedding in the park.

INTERVENE

To come between.

The great powers tried to intervene between the Arabs and the Israelis to bring peace to the Middle East.

AVENUE

The path or road by which one came, a broad roadway.

Fifth Avenue in midtown New York City is a great center for shopping.

INVENTORY

An itemized list of the goods in stock.

The department store had a huge sale to reduce its inventory before the end of the season.

COVENANT

A solemn mutual agreement.

The covenant of the League of Nations tried to promote disarmament and international cooperation.

CONVENT

A place where a community of nuns live.

Sister Mary left the convent every morning to go to work in the city hospital.

PREVENT

To come before, to hinder, to stop from happening.

She held her child's hand firmly to prevent him from running into the street.

CONVENIENT

Not troublesome, suitable, agreeable.

They found the location of their new apartment very convenient because it was close to transportation and shopping.

VENTURE

A risky undertaking.

He loved to cook, so when he retired from teaching he opened up a restaurant, but his business venture failed because of his lack of experience.

REVENUE

The income coming in from your possessions.

The New York City government complains that its revenue from taxes is insufficient and asks for more state and federal aid.

SOUVENIR

Something that calls up memories, a keepsake.

They bought small gift items in each city they visited to keep as souvenirs of their trip.

VERT VERS

Meaning: To turn.

Origin: Latin, *vertere*, to turn.

All our communication media—radio, TV, newspapers, magazines—are loaded with ADVERTISEMENTS designed to induce us to buy an enormous array of products, ranging from toothpaste and breakfast cereals, to cars, washing machines, and airline flights. Advertising is a gigantic industry; nowadays, hardly any product can succeed without it.

Advertising appeals to the highest instincts in man, as well as to the basest: how to get rich, smart, beautiful, healthy, successful; how to keep up with the Joneses, get ahead of the Joneses; how to find pleasure, excitement, romance, adventure.

Without advertising, we might save a lot of money we spend uselessly, but we might also remain ignorant of useful information about products.

DIVERSE, DIVERSIFIED

Different, varied.

He is a man with diverse interests and enjoys everything from opera to soccer.

CONVERSE

The opposite.

She loves cats, but unfortunately the converse is not true and cats do not love her.

DIVERSION

Amusement, pastime, distraction.

A popular diversion of young people when they are tired of doing homework is television.

AVERT

To turn away from, to avoid.

At the movies, Mary would avert her eyes from the scenes with violence and bloodshed.

DIVERT

To turn aside, to distract the attention of.

A sudden loud noise at the back of the theater diverted the audience's attention from the play.

DIVERT

To amuse, entertain.

The babysitter diverted the child by reading him the comics.

VERTIGO

Dizziness.

The couple whirled round and round as they danced until they began to experience a sensation of vertigo.

INVERT

To turn upside down.

She inverted the can of dog food to remove the contents.

INTROVERT

One who turns his mind upon himself.

Introverts are usually shy, quiet, and withdrawn and are uncomfortable in social situations.

INVERSE

Turned in an opposite direction.

The school psychologist reported that John's poor grades were in inverse relation to his high I.Q.

CONTROVERSY

A dispute, a discussion with sharp differences of opinion, a debate.

The controversy over slavery in the United States culminated in the Civil War between the North and the South.

PERVERT

To turn from what is true, right, natural; to lead astray; to corrupt; to distort.

The pornographic movie perverted sex into something ugly, commercial, and sinful.

CONVERT

To change.

They sold their car and converted their garage into a playroom.

To exchange.

When they got to London, they converted their dollars into pounds.

To adopt a different religion.

She was born Jewish, but converted to Catholicism when she married a Catholic.

ADVERSARY

An opponent, enemy.

The candidate claimed that his adversary in the presidential election lacked sufficient experience.

EXTROVERT

A person who is outgoing, who mingles easily with people.

John is an extrovert and loves to go to parties and be with people.

AVERSION

Intense dislike.

She was bitten by a dog when she was a child and has had an aversion to dogs ever since.

VERSATILE

Able to turn his hand successfully to many different things.

An artist, sculptor, scientist, Leonardo da Vinci was probably the most versatile genius the world has ever known.

REVERT

To turn back.

One of the major problems of criminology is how to rehabilitate prisoners so they will not revert to crime.

REVERSE

Change to the opposite direction or order.

First they turned to the right, but it was wrong, so they reversed and went to the left.

The back.

Her name was on one side of the locket, and her birthdate was on the reverse side.

ADVERSE

Unfavorable, harmful.

It rained almost every day, but the adverse weather did not spoil their vacation.

SUBVERT

To overthrow, to undermine, to corrupt.

Joseph McCarthy accused many people of trying to subvert the United States government.

VERTEBRATE

Having a backbone or spinal column.

There are five classes of vertebrates: fish, amphibians, birds, reptiles, and mammals.

VERTICAL

Upright, straight up and down, perpendicular to a horizontal plane.

After sitting over his studies for hours, he found it a relief to take a vertical position and stand up and walk around.

VERSE

Poetry, words arranged in meter or rhyme.

She made a card for his birthday and wrote an original verse with her greetings.

VERSION

Translation.

There are many different versions of the Bible.

An account showing one particular point of view.

They both read the same book but their versions of it differ a great deal.

VERSUS

Against.

In the case of Brown versus the Topeka, Kansas, Board of Education, the Supreme Court of the United States made a historic decision against segregation.

V I D   V I S

Meaning: To see.

Origin: Latin, *videre*, to see.

VISION, *the ability to take in external stimuli through the eyes,* is one of the most important means of adaptation and learning. But there were men who were not satisfied with ordinary sight. They wanted to perceive that which was not apparent to the naked eye.

A Dutchman, Anton von Leeuwenhoek, had a mania for making the world's most perfect microscopes. He looked at everything imaginable through these fine lenses. One day, he saw thousands of bacteria swimming in drops of rain water. For the first time, a man saw the world of little beasts who, despite their size, were so mighty they could kill beings a hundred million times as big as they. Leeuwenhoek gave the first complete description of these animalcules, as he called them—the bacteria and protozoa.

Another man who sought to extend man's vision, literally and figuratively, was Galileo, who made the first telescope. This invention brought the heavens millions of miles closer to us. The whole expanse of the universe was now open to the inquiring gaze of man. With his telescope, Galileo proved the truth of Copernicus' theory that the sun, and not the earth, was at the center of the universe.

PROVIDE

To supply.

*The hotel provided a room
with breakfast, but no other
meals.*

PROVIDE

To arrange means of support,
to take care for the future.

*They saved up enough money
to provide for their old age.*

VIEW

What is seen, a scene or sight.

On a clear day, the view of New York City from the top of the Empire State Building is magnificent.

Way of looking at something, idea, opinion.

The union held an open forum about which candidate to endorse for president, and all the members were invited to express their views before a general decision was made.

EVIDENT

Easy to see, clear, plain.

The evidence presented by the district attorney was overwhelming and it was evident to the jury that the man was guilty.

VIS-À-VIS

Literally, face to face.

Instead of sitting next to each other on the train, they sat vis-à-vis so that they could play cards.

In relation to.

The politician refused to make any statement vis-à-vis the accusation that he had accepted bribes.

PREVIEW

A private showing before something is exhibited to the public.

The people who attended the preview of the show did not like it, so the opening was postponed and revisions were made.

VISA

A stamp put on a document, usually a passport, giving permission to travel to a particular country.

When we were in Greece, we decided it would be nice to go to Yugoslavia, but we did not have a visa.

SUPERVISE

To oversee, to direct workers.

The department head super-vised the employees to see that the work was done correctly and on time.

VISIBLE

Can be seen.

The footprints under the window were a visible sign that someone had entered the house.

REVISE

To look at again, to correct, to change, to bring up to date.

Textbooks on science have to be revised every few years because of new discoveries.

EVIDENCE

Facts presented in a court of law.

Although they established that the gun used in the murder belonged to him, this was regarded as circumstantial evidence since no one could prove he had actually fired it.

Indication, sign.

The horse had given no evidence of being in good form and everyone was amazed when it won the race.

REVIEW

To look at again, to go over, to reexamine.

Before the final examination, the teacher reviewed the work of the semester.

To discuss critically.

The newspaper review of the new movie praised the actors but said the plot was ridiculous.

INVISIBLE

Cannot be seen.

Until the invention of the microscope, germs that caused many illnesses were not identifiable because they were invisible.

VISIT

To go to see, to pay a call, to spend some time with.

The newlyweds go to visit their in-laws every Friday night.

V I A

Meaning: Road, way.

Origin: Latin, *via*, road, way

A VOYAGE is a *journey over considerable distance.* It usually involves travel over water.

Probably the most famous single voyage in all of world history was Columbus's journey to America. Of course, Columbus did not so much discover America as stumble upon it. He never realized the great discovery he had made, believing to his dying day that he had reached India.

Because of Columbus's mistake, we use the same word for the Indian of America and for the Indian of India.

PREVIOUS

Going or occurring before.

When John started his new job, he was told that the previous bookkeeper had left a mess that he would have to straighten out.

OBVIOUS

Easy to see or understand, clear, plain.

When they opened their door, it was obvious that their apartment had been broken into.

VIADUCT

An elevated, arch-supported structure carrying a roadway— usually over a valley.

Viaducts are usually built in mountainous country.

DEVIATE

To turn aside.

He stuck to his plan and never once deviated from it.

IMPERVIOUS

Not allowing anything to pass through.

A good raincoat is impervious to the rain.

Not affected or influenced by.

He had made up his mind to drop out of school and was impervious to reason or argument.

DEVIOUS

Crooked, winding.

To throw the cops off his trail, the escaped prisoner took a devious route through the forest.

Not straightforward.

The workers do not trust the foreman because he is very devious in reporting what they do to the boss.

V O C V O K

Meaning: To call.

Origin: Latin, *vocare*, to call.
Latin, *vox*, the voice.

A fancy word for *a trade, profession,* or *occupation* is VOCATION. Ordinarily, one thinks of working at a job merely as a way of making a living. But the word VOCATION carries an additional meaning. It suggests that one is responding to an inner call, or feels summoned to a particular kind of work.

It is deeply satisfying to perform well on a job, especially if it is one we chose to do out of enjoyment. Unfortunately, taking pride in one's work seems to be an outmoded virtue in our highly mechanized society. Nevertheless, people still strive to work at jobs they enjoy. The aim of vocational guidance is to direct people toward careers suitable to their abilities and interests.

The original meaning of the word VOCATION, or *calling,* was a religious one. In the Catholic Church, if a young man showed great interest and devotion to the Church, people would say he had "a sure vocation," meaning that he felt a call to become a priest.

AVOCATION

What one does for amusement, for relaxation, away from one's regular occupation, a hobby.

A group of doctors at the hospital whose avocation was playing musical instruments got together and formed a small orchestra.

EQUIVOCAL

Capable of two different interpretations, purposely vague or ambiguous; literally, it means speaking with two equal voices.

When the candidate was asked what his position was with regard to the abortion issue, his answer was equivocal.

VOCIFEROUS

Making a loud outcry, shouting noisily.

When the department store refused to give him a refund, he became vociferous and they had to call the store police to quiet him down.

VOCABULARY

A list of words with their meanings; all the words of a language; all the words a particular person knows.

A good way to improve your vocabulary is to learn about word roots.

INVOKE

To call upon in prayer, to beg for.

The condemned prisoner invoked the mercy of the judge.

To call forth by magic.

The spiritualist invoked the spirit of the dead.

ADVOCATE

One who pleads the cause of another; a counselor.

The jury was impressed by the advocate's forceful presentation of the defendant's case.

To speak in favor of.

The senator advocated reducing the military budget and increasing aid to education.

PROVOKE

To call forth, to bring about, to cause.

The controversial movie about the war in Viet Nam provoked a lot of discussion.

To make angry, to irritate.

The child would not take no for an answer and finally provoked his father into punishing him.

REVOKE

To call back, to withdraw, to cancel.

His driving license was revoked because he is a reckless driver and has had many traffic violations.

CONVOKE

To call together, to summon to meet, to convene.

The President convoked a meeting of top physicians to advise him on national health policy.

IRREVOCABLE

Cannot be called back or undone, unalterable.

No matter how they pleaded with him, his decision to quit was irrevocable.

EVOKE

To call forth, to bring out.

The speaker's statement that he favored a reduction in taxes evoked applause from the audience.

VOICE

Sound made through the mouth in talking or singing.

The baby awoke suddenly and started crying, but stopped as soon as he heard his mother's voice.

The right to express one's ideas.

In a democracy, everyone can have a voice in making government policy.

VOCAL

Uttered or formed by the voice.

The vocal powers of the opera singer, Enrico Caruso, were legendary.

V O L V

Meaning: To roll.

Origin: Latin, *volvere*, to roll.

A REVOLUTION means *a complete rolling about*. In a literal sense, one complete revolution of the earth around the sun takes a year.

The word REVOLUTION is also used in a different sense. In this case, the "complete rolling about" signifies *a complete or drastic change*. This kind of revolution can involve violence, as when a government is overthrown by war. The American Revolution of 1776, the French Revolution of 1789, and the Russian Revolution of 1917 all brought about complete changes in government.

Though a revolution always brings change, it is not always violent. A revolution can sometimes come about through thought rather than through action. Inventions such as the telephone, the car, the airplane, and many others, have revolutionized contemporary living. The ideas of scientists such as Newton, Pasteur, Einstein, and Salk have stimulated revolutionary changes.

A very important bloodless revolution took place in the second half of the eighteenth century. The Industrial Revolution marked a complete change in the way goods were produced. Before, things were made by hand, and the outlay of money and time was enormous. With the Industrial Revolution came the machinery which was capable of cheaply producing vast quantities of goods. The Industrial Revolution ushered in the age of technology. Today, even the poor can enjoy luxuries that the kings of yesterday did not dream of.

REVOLTING

Disgusting, offensive, repulsive.

Mary's mother is old-fashioned and finds Mary's tastes in clothes, in music, and in dancing altogether revolting.

CONVOLUTE

To roll, twist, or coil together

The boa constrictor is a gigantic snake which kills by convoluting itself around the victim's body.

REVOLVE

To go around.

In order to enter the hotel, the little boy pushed the door to make it revolve.

VOLUME

Originally, a roll of parchment; one of the books in a set.

He has a complete set of the works of Charles Dickens in 15 volumes.

A mass, large quantity, loudness.

We always have to ask our neighbors to please turn down the volume when they play their TV.

REVOLVER

A pistol with a revolving mechanism in which a number of bullets may be placed.

The policeman kept firing his revolver at the escaping robber until he ran out of bullets and had to reload.

EVOLUTION

The theory that all species of plants and animals developed from earlier forms.

When Charles Darwin published his theory of evolution in 1858, people who believed that each species was created separately by God were outraged.

REVOLT

To rise up against, to refuse to submit to authority.

The students revolted against the increase in tuition fees.

EVOLVE

To roll out, to unfold, to develop gradually.

The police set the trap for the suspect and then they waited to see what would evolve.

DEVOLVE

Literally, to roll down upon, to fall to another person.

When the father died, the care of the family devolved upon the oldest son.

INVOLVE

Include.

Mary's work for the school newspaper involved interviewing the new teachers and writing about them for the paper.

Occupy.

John was deeply involved in doing his homework and forgot all about time.

INDEX

INDEX

Root words appear in italics.

attention, 307
attractive, 322
au courant, 73
autocracy, 66
automobile, 182
autonomy, 185
avenue, 332
aversion, 337
avocation, 345
avoid, 325

Ball, 149
bank, 39
bankrupt, 252, 253
barometer, 172
bell, 24
bellicose, 24
belligerent, 24
bench, 39
benediction, 86
bibliomania, 161
bibliophile, 211
bicycle, 79
biology, 157
bisect, 263
bishop, 256
blanch, 39
blank, 39
bonafide, 108

Cacophony, 216
cad, 25
cadaver, 25
cadence, 27
cadenza, 26
canal, 31
cand, 28
candelabrum, 28
candid, 30
candidate, 28, 30
candle, 28
candor, 29
cane, 30, 32
caneh, 31

canister, 32
cannon, 31, 32
canon, 31, 33
canonize, 31
canyon, 32
cap, 34
capable, 35
capacious, 35
capacity, 38
capit, 39
capital, 42
capitulate, 42
caps, 43
capsule, 43
captain, 39, 41
captivate, 37
captive, 36
capture, 36
carcinogen, 117
cas, 25
case, 27, 43, 44
cash, 44
casket, 44
cassette, 43
castle, 40
caveat, 92
cease, 45
cede, 45
ceed, 45
centipede, 195
cept, 34
cern, 50
cert, 50
certain, 51
certificate, 50
certify, 51
cess, 45
chance, 27
chandelier, 29
channel, 31, 33
chapter, 40
chateau, 40
chef, 39, 41
chief, 39
chief, 41
chisel, 55
chron, 52

chronic, 53
chronicle, 52, 53
chronological, 53
chronometer, 52
cid, 25
cide, 54
circle, 81
circuit, 139
circular, 79
circulate, 82
circumcise, 55
circumspect, 283
circus, 80
cis, 54
cit, 57
citation, 58
cite, 59
claim, 61
claimant, 62
clam, 60
clamor, 60
claus, 63
clause, 64
claustrophobia, 64, 214
close, 65
closet, 64
clud, 63
clus, 63
cognition, 125
cognoscenti, 124
coincide, 26
coincidence, 27
coincident, 27
collate, 148
colleague, 151
collect, 150
collection, 150
colloquial, 159
command, 165
commemorate, 169
commend, 165
commensurate, 171
comment, 169
commission, 175
commit, 175
committee, 174
commotion, 184

evolve, 350
example, 92
exceed, 46
except, 36
excited, 58
exclaim, 61
exclude, 63, 65
exclusive, 63, 64
excursion, 74
execute, 271
executioner, 271
executive, 271
executor, 271
exempt, 93
exit, 138
expedient, 194
expedite, 196
expedition, 195
expel, 199
expend, 205
expense, 202, 207
expensive, 206
expire, 286, 287
explicit, 220
exponent, 225
export, 231
expose, 226
exposition, 225
express, 235
expunge, 239
extend, 308
extensive, 309
extent, 307
extort, 319
extract, 323
extraction, 9
extrovert, 336

Fab, 101
fable, 101
fabulous, 102
facilitate, 100
facility, 98
facsimile, 99
fact, 97
fact, 100

faction, 99
factor, 100
factory, 97, 99
faith, 107
fam, 101
famous, 102
fant, 101
fate, 103
feat, 99
feature, 99
fect, 97
fer, 104
fertile, 104
fertilize, 106
fid, 107
fidelity, 107, 109
fiduciary, 107
fingerprint, 234
flect, 110
flex, 110
flex, 111
flexible, 110
footprint, 236
found, 115
foundation, 115
founder, 115
Founding Fathers, 115
foundry, 112
fratricide, 54, 56
fund, 112, 115
fund, 116
fundamental, 116
funnel, 113
fus, 112
fuse, 114
fusion, 112

Gender, 119
gene, 119
genealogy, 118
general, 118
generation, 118
generous, 121
genesis, 117
genial, 119
genital, 119

genius, 120
genocide, 55, 119
genre, 117
genus, 117
geo, 122
geocentric, 122
geography, 123
geology, 123
geometry, 122
geopolitics, 123
george, 123
geriatrics, 136
gnosis, 124
gnosticism, 124
grad, 126
grade, 127
gradual, 126
graduate, 126
gram, 129
grammar, 130
graph, 129
graph, 130
graphic, 130
greg, 132
gregarious, 132
gres, 126

Heliophobia, 214
hemophilia, 212
heterogeneous, 120
hierarchy, 22
hiss, 187
homage, 134
homicide, 54
homogeneous, 120
homogenize, 120
homonym, 188
horoscope, 257
human, 134, 135
humane, 135
humble, 135
humiliate, 134
humus, 134
humus, 135
hydrogen, 119
hydrophobia, 213

mortgage, 180
mortician, 181
mortify, 181
mot, 182
motion, 184
motive, 184
motorcycle, 80
mov, 182
movement, 182
multiply, 221
murder, 181

Nemesis, 185
neolithic, 154
nice, 57
nomos, 185
non sequitur, 273
nonsense, 269

Oath, 138
obituary, 140
object, 143
obstetrician, 291
obstruct, 296
obvious, 343
occasion, 26
occasional, 26
occident, 25, 27
occlude, 63
occur, 71, 74
offer, 104
onoma, 187
onomatopoeic, 187
opponent, 227
opportune, 231
opportunity, 231
oppose, 223

opposite, 227
oppress, 13, 235
ortho, 190
orthodontia, 190
orthodox, 190
orthography, 190
orthopedist, 190, 196
osteopath, 192

Pachyderm, 84
paleolithic, 154
parasympathetic, 191
parenthesis, 311
participate, 37
pass, 191
passion, 193
passive, 193
path, 191
pathetic, 192
pathology, 192
pathos, 193
patience, 193
patriarch, 22
patronymic, 189
ped, 194, 196
pedagogue, 197
pedal, 195
pedantic, 197
pedestal, 195
pedestrian, 194
pediatrician, 136, 196
pedicure, 77
pedigree, 195
pel, 198
pend, 202
pendulous, 205
pendulum, 204
pensive, 205

perambulator, 20
perception, 37
peremptory, 92
perfidy, 108
perimeter, 170
periscope, 258
perjure, 144
permit, 175
perpendicular, 204
perpetual, 209
perplex, 220
persecute, 273
persist, 277
perspective, 283
perspicacity, 285
perspire, 287
peso, 202
pet, 208
petition, 209
petulant, 209
phil, 211
philanderer, 212
philanthropist, 211
philatelist, 212
philharmonic, 212
philippic, 211
Phillip, 211
philology, 212
philosophy, 212
philter, 212
phobia, 213
phobia, 213
phon, 215
phonetics, 216
phonograph, 131, 215
pliable, 220
pliant, 220
plic, 217
pliers, 219

salacious, 255
sally, 255
sample, 93
sandwich, 14
saw, 262
scent, 268
scop, 256
scope, 257
scrib, 259
scribble, 260
scribe, 260
script, 259
script, 261
scriptures, 261
scythe, 263
seat, 265
sec, 262
secede, 47
seclude, 65
section, 264
sector, 264
secure, 77
sed, 265
sedatives, 265, 266
sedentary, 265
sediment, 265
sedition, 139
seduce, 91
segment, 263
segregation, 132
select, 150
semper fidelis, 108
send, 270
sens, 268
sensation, 268
sense, 269
sensible, 270
sensitive, 269
sensual, 270

sensuous, 270
sent, 268
sentence, 268
sentiment, 269
sequ, 271
sequel, 273
sequence, 272
sess, 265
session, 266
set, 267
settle, 266
shekel, 202
sickle, 263
sign, 274
signal, 274
signature, 275
signet, 274
significant, 276
signify, 276
silly, 57
simple, 219
sinecure, 75
sist, 277
sit, 266
soliloquy, 159
solu, 279
soluble, 279
solution, 280
solv, 279
solve, 280
solvent, 279
somersault, 254
somnambulist, 20
spec, 282
specimen, 283
spectacle, 284
spectacular, 283
spectator, 282
specter, 284

spectrum, 284
speculate, 283
speedometer, 171
spend, 202
spire, 286
spirit, 286, 288
sport, 231
sprightly, 287
sprite, 288
sta, 289
stability, 289
stable, 290
state, 291
static, 292
station, 291
stationary, 293
stationery, 290
statistics, 293
statue, 289
stature, 290
status, 292
statute, 292
stay, 291
stethoscope, 256
stipend, 203
strike, 149
struct, 294
structures, 294
subject, 143
submit, 174
subscribe, 261
subtract, 324
subvert, 337
sue, 273
suffer, 106
suffuse, 114
suicide, 54
suitable, 273
suite, 272